WORKING WITH PARENTS
AND INFANTS

WORKING WITH PARENTS AND INFANTS

A Mind-Body Integration Approach

Antonella Sansone

KARNAC

First published in 2007 by
Karnac Books Ltd
118 Finchley Road
London NW3 5HT

British Library Cataloguing in Publication Data

A.C.I.P. for this book is available from the British Library

ISBN-13: 978-1-85575-438-6

Designed, and produced by HL Studios, Long Hanborough, Oxford

www.karnacbooks.com

Contents

To my dancing daughter Gisele and to her loving father David

About the author

Antonella Sansone is a doctor of Clinical Psychology and has a Master Degree in psychoanalytical observational studies. She is also a baby massage practitioner.

The author is a research and clinical psychologist particularly interested in pre and postnatal life. She is also a yoga practitioner and this reflects her belief in the importance of the mind and body unity and balance as foundation of health. As a baby massage teacher, she believes that mindful massage for infants has the potential to regulate the mother-baby psychobiological rhythms and thus be a vital part of the bonding process and a reassuring extension of the womb environment.

Acknowledgements

I would like to thank the infants and their parents who taught me so much about infant pre-verbal communication, the complex interactions between them, and the development of emotions. Thanks to them, I trained to become able to feel and observe my emotions and cope with different kinds of anxieties, some related to a kind of rebirth, others arising from facing a new experience.

Using English, my second language, often meant that I called on my body language, a more child-like language, which has helped me communicate with infants. These experiences sharpened my observational skills, my capacity to listen to, and feel "compassion" for the difficulties of parents and infants. Without these experiences, I would probably not have been able to heal the difficulties of the mother and infant presented in this book.

I am grateful to Vezio Ruggieri, Professor of Psycho-Physiology at the Department of Psychology at Rome University "La Sapienza", for his invaluable integrated model, to which this book refers extensively. I have benefited enormously from his integrative view of psychological phenomena in developing a research project on a woman's bodyself image and its effects on pregnancy, birth, and early interactions with the baby, and as the beneficiary of the Leonardo da Vinci Fellowship.

I thank the Birth Unit of St John and St Elizabeth Hospital for providing a unique observational setting through prenatal and post-natal classes, thus giving me a unique learning opportunity.

My thanks also go to Yehudi Gordon, consultant obstetrician at the Birth Unit and the pioneer of water birthing in the UK, who was consistently available when feedback was needed. He invariably demonstrated a lively interest in my observations.

I am especially grateful to Peter Walker, the pioneer of baby massage in the UK, for providing unique observational settings for observing early mother-infant interactions. While observing Peter Walker's classes, I made a life-changing discovery. In terms of academic and clinical knowledge, I greatly value his extensive practical experience with parents and infants and my experiential study in his classes. By acting as an integrated expression of caring that contributes to both physical and psychological healing for both babies and parents, baby massage is a complementary tool in psychotherapeutic work with parents and infants.

I should like to thank the Tavistock Clinic / University of East London, as this book arose out of my master's dissertation. The infant observation seminar and the work discussion, fundamental components of the MA in Psychoanalytical Observational Studies, were invaluable sources of inspiration in my work with the mother and infant discussed here, and in the writing of this book. My observational skills have been sharpened by the experience of infant observation. This experience gave me a unique opportunity to develop my ability to feel the emotions aroused during the observations, to look at my inner feelings and to observe those of the mother and infant, and to reflect upon them.

Special thanks to Dr Judith Trowell, who supervised my master's dissertation and gave me invaluable feedback.

I also owe so much to my regular yoga practice and the teachings of Eastern approaches in the therapeutic and healing relationship between therapist and client. They have provided me with insights about how to creatively integrate them into Western theories and approaches in my work with parents and infants.

Heartfelt thanks to my husband David for his help in looking after our child Gisele while I was writing this book, since she was a few days old, and for his warm support.

I would also like to express my gratitude to my mum, who flew from Italy and spent a month with us, helping me with Gisele and thus contributing to the writing of this book.

Most importantly, heartfelt thanks to little Gisele, as her fairly settled sleeping patterns, almost since birth, and joyful nature, have allowed me to work on this book during her sleep. I would have struggled to write it if she had not been the way she is.

Introduction

> A subsidiary task in infant development is that of psychosomatic indwelling...Much of the physical part of the infant care–holding, handling, bathing, feeding, and so on–is designed to facilitate the baby's achievement of a psyche-soma that lives and works in harmony with itself. (Winnicott, 1967, p. 29).

Central to this book is an examination of the ways in which the unconscious life of the mind expresses itself through a woman's body, and conversely, the manner in which the body's experiences impinge upon the mind. This was greatly illuminated by Dinora Pines, who enabled us to see how the secrets of the mind and body can move into conscious awareness in the analytical setting, and find a space there for thought and change (Pines, 1993).

Our early life is a cascade of sensory experiences: of sight, sounds, smells, and experiences of touch and movement. Drawing on a single case of a difficult mother-infant relationship, combined with infant observations, psychoanalytical thought, and work in neighbouring disciplines, I shall consider how early experiences of touch and movement become stored in the body, and how such experiences may be acted out in adult life and affect the early mother-infant relationship. Pregnancy and childbirth are a crucial time for parents, since they reactivate unresolved issues, which, left untreated, can develop into more complex chronic conditions or even pathology.

In contrast to the "dualism" of Western science and medicine, I argue for the inseparability of psyche and soma. Beyond this, I am particularly interested in the embodiment of emotional health– as well as of emotional illness–and in their origins in our earliest experiences.

This book thus concerns the field of early emotions in all of us. The human body has long been excluded from psychological and relational processes. The widely held view that any illness or difficulty should be classified as either "mental" or "physical" has long been predominant. This is partly related to conventional and religious factors, in particular to Cartesian dualism (Bermúdez,

Marcel, & Eilan, 1995). Classic neurology considers the muscular system as a mechanism at the service of the mind. However, the mind plays a major role in whatever we are doing. A healthy, well-functioning mind can make effective use of information from the body and displays itself via the body in a feedback relationship. Could we express a loving gesture, such as a kiss or hug, without the muscles that enable us to produce it? And if the muscles involved in these gestures have excessive tension, how can the message be communicated clearly?

These central psychosomatic issues, viewed from an object-relations perspective, link my work particularly to that of D. W. Winnicott, D. Pines, and to theory emerging from psychoanalytic observation of infants and from other child development research.

My interest in the psychoanalytic significance of touch and movement is related primarily to my work as a prenatal and post-natal psychologist and baby massage practitioner in a Hospital Birth Unit. I shall explore baby massage in terms of object relations, as an integral part of psychotherapy. I have found that parent and infant engagement in such activity is emotionally significant. It may restage primal experiences of touch and movement in the parent, which can parallel other significant changes in the course of psychotherapy. Links between the emotional and physical experiences of baby massage and memories of early life emerge. This understanding can strengthen a parent's ability to change things in the present. Object-relations theory offers the possibility of exploring the evolution of the mother's repertoire of gestures, massage movement, physical holding, and her relationship to her inner world of feelings in the context of early infantile experiences.

Chapter 1 is entitled A Historical Examination of The Psyche-Soma. This chapter explores some theoretical gaps concerning psychoanalytical thinking with regards to the psyche-soma. The ideas I present are aimed at understanding the process of psychosomatic illness and at exploring the embodiment of psychosomatic health and illness. I will highlight the beneficial function of psychosomatic symptoms, such as mastitis, in signalling to the counsellor or therapist (as well as the patient), the need for change and the path through which it may occur. Mastitis is an inflammation of the breast whose cause is "unknown" by science. It develops when breast milk is not flowing well and can be very painful. It is ascribed to unusual events that interrupt normal patterns of feeding, for example, returning to work for the first time, going out to an exciting event, such as a party, or disruption of the mother's feeding pattern due to travel. It seems to me that a dualistic perspective prevents recognising that the mother's concerns, conflicts, and mental state can equally obstruct the flow of milk and affect the infant's feeding patterns–indeed the mother-infant relationship at all levels.

In the case discussed in this book (involving a mother named Andrea), mastitis was treated primarily as a medical problem by the midwives and the consultant obstetrician. I developed the approach, however, that mastitis was not Andrea's central problem, but a "symptom", a mind/body strategy to avoid physical contact with her baby, which would have stirred unbearable anxieties in the mother. This was consistent with Andreas's tendency to leave the baby with me or with the midwife who assisted in her labour and delivery. I draw on a single case to illustrate how some mothers, who have had damaged relationships with their own mothers, struggle to solve their own mother-child conflicts and how these conflicts can manifest through psychosomatic disturbance.

The mother-infant relationship provides the first context for experiences of touch or "handling" (Winnicott, 1960b). It is also the setting for early movements and thus for the sense of proprioception (the sense that informs us of the current position, speed, and direction of movement of our body parts.) One of the baby's earliest interests is the exploration of his or her mother's body. For instance, the breast is the baby's primary object, which "stands for" the mother, and through breastfeeding, babies have a learning experience of themselves as well as of their mothers. I assume that these early experiences impinge on the development of a grounded bodyself, and on the way a mother uses her body and its expressions in interacting with her baby. In early life, touch, movement, and emotions are intimately related. Through movement and gesture, often combined with vocalization and eye contact, the infant signals a desire for interaction. So does the mother, and in doing so, she reinforces the infant's initiations and responses. Andrea's baby was missing these earliest experiences of maternal touch and this became evident in her lack of vital movement and inert body.

In Chapter 2, I endeavour to consider Winnicott's vision of the psyche-soma and Pine's thinking on the ways in which the mind expresses itself through a woman's body, and conversely, the manner in which it is affected by the body's experiences. I shall also set these ideas into a broader psychoanalytic context. Largely speaking, physical activities have not been addressed by psychoanalysis (McDougall, 1989). It seems to me that a dualistic framework, together with a tendency to focus more upon illness that upon health, underpins an "either/or" perspective.

On the same line as Winnicott's vision of the psyche-soma, I argue that somatic aspects of self-expression and communication play a useful and essential part in everyday life. They play a major part in the mother-infant relationship. Baby massage in particular has offered me an interesting setting for observing how Andrea handled her baby, her gestures, and body language. Somatic aspects become problematic when the harmony and unity of the psyche-soma has been impaired, i.e. when body and self are split and the body is experienced as an object rather than as the venue of the self. This results in psychosomatic symptoms, psychological difficulties, or self-injury. I underpin the importance of acknowledging the continuum between health and illness in order to understand the subjective meaning and function of symptoms, as they inform the therapist of a divorce between psyche and soma.

The psyche-soma in health is, for Winnicott (1949), an inseparable unity. A split between them is for him a basis for disturbance. His work is therefore a precious base for considering psychosomatic processes and, in particular, their beneficial function. Winnicott's thinking often illuminates the clinical case presented, in this instance, my understanding of the meaning of mastitis and Andrea's "subjective" use of it.

In his work on the psyche-soma, Winnicott suggested that experiences of touch and movement profoundly affect our sense of "psychosomatic indwelling" (Winnicott 1967). For him, a sense of "true self" evolved within bodily experiences and was rooted in the body. I have noticed that psychosomatic symptoms are commonly accompanied by other somatic changes as well as by an impoverishment of verbal self-expression. This was evident in Andrea's tightened gestures while breastfeeding, her remarkably fast and sharp way of speaking, and in her inability to verbalize her feelings and her internal world.

In Chapter 3, I suggest that the mother's attitude to her bodily and mental space, thus her attitude to the bodyself, affects the child's sense of an integrated bodyself image. Research and clinical literature has paid very little attention to how a woman's bodyself image may impinge upon her parental skills and on the quality of interactions with her baby. When the mother's integrated bodyself image and her associated self-confidence enable her to receive and contain the baby's fears, crying, and anger, giving her back these feelings in a renewed light rather than rejecting them, she allows her baby to acknowledge them through a mirroring process. If this process does not take place, the infant may escape from the frightening feelings and become unable to monitor them in later life. When the mother produces resistance, which hinders her from connecting with her emotions and inner child, her baby will have difficulty receiving back his or her own feelings and thus developing an integrated bodyself image based on a true experience of self.

In Chapter 4, I explore more widely the subject of touch and movement. I present and discuss a clinical example of the beneficial use of baby massage classes as an integral part of psychotherapeutic work with parents and infants. I highlight the significance of the presence of the third person–the infant massage teacher–as a containing, mindful object for the projected anxiety, depression, or even more primitive states. I then consider how infant massage may help restore a sense of psychosomatic indwelling in the mother as well as smooth its evolution in the baby. For Winnicott such indwelling was the home for a true self, a source of authenticity and enjoyment.

I am aware that where baby massage, complementary remedies, or therapies in general are concerned, it is vital to consider whether its practice encourages a belief in illusory solutions to a problem. When difficulties between mother and infant occur, baby massage can be beneficial as a useful tool in psychotherapeutic work, and conversely, psychoanalysis can enhance the benefits, and experience, of baby massage at all levels. Its playfulness and the experience of touch involved can also help the mother and infant recover from psychosomatic distress.

One aim of this book is to bring into sharper focus the ways in which a baby and mother interact and change each other. When change occurs for better in the relationship between parent and baby, then parenting becomes easier and more enjoyable; the baby thrives. Old cycles of intergenerational problems can be broken and replaced by healthy parent-child and family relationships.

Drawing on clinical material, on Winnicott's work, and from other ideas from child development research and psychoanalysis, I endeavour to enhance the understanding of the vital importance of the touch experience during baby massage in restoring the damaged integration of the psyche-soma. It is relevant that in popular culture, mind and body are regarded as two sides of the same coin. As the oldest and the most natural of all the healing arts, baby massage has been practiced to ease childbirth, aid recovery, soothe babies, and provide a remedy in many cultures the world over.

In Chapter 5, I illustrate a troubled mother-infant relationship, giving a description of how a lack of being "held" as a child may cause a mother's intolerance of physical contact with her baby and how this can manifest through developing a psychosomatic disturbance or symptom. In the clinical case illustrated, I have changed identifying details, without distorting the essentials. Therefore, if a reader finds similarities to someone known, this can be considered as coincidence, or more likely, a sign of the commonness of the phenomenon described. In Andrea's case, her mastitis (a breast inflammation that may prevent a woman from breastfeeding) was treated as a medical problem by the midwives. It appeared to me, however, to be a "symptom', a mind/body strategy to avoid physical contact with her baby and thus the overwhelming emotions aroused by it. Mastitis, like other manifestations of the mother's use of her body, is seen in this book as the symptom of a psychosomatic dysfunction. In this book, it is conceived as the expression of a conflict between the mother's idealistic idea of breastfeeding and thus her will to accomplish it, and her inability to cope with the intense feelings stirred up by it.

In Chapter 6, I present a new approach to health and the healing relationship, emerging from a meeting between Eastern meditative disciplines and Western psychological practice. My regular practice of meditation and yoga helped me to heal Andrea's difficulties from inside herself as well as inside the relationship with her baby. I shall highlight the importance of the therapist's "empathic perception" for the healing process. I consider how my aim was to work with the mother on her past, not in a theoretical way, but through her body awareness, thus through her actual relationship with her baby.

On the same line as Buddhist philosophy, "well-being" is conceived in terms of the full union of mind and body, not in the negative meaning of absence of sickness. I consider the positive function of a symptom in guiding the therapist, as well as the client, in re-establishing the unity of mind and body. In Western psychology a symptom is often considered to be the "problem" and it is believed that well-being depends on getting rid of it. As the mother-infant case illustrated in this book shows, my aim was not to suppress the mastitis symptom, the "faraway" quality of the mother's language, or her lack of eye contact, etc, but to guide her to a new awareness or enlightenment, growing out of a complete transformation.

In Chapter 7, I suggest that to understand the importance and effectiveness of early support, we need to adapt a new neuropsychological theory of emotions. Central to this new theory is the notion that healthy bonding relationships with the primary caregivers shape healthy brains and efficient connections of neurons in the brain. The hypothalamus is closely connected to the limbic system and together they form the locus of emotional centres. They form a complex network that can be conceived as a "primal adaptive system." The right hemisphere in particular contains an integrated map of the bodily state and plays a major role in the regulation of fundamental physiological and hormonal functions. Since the hypothalamus-pituitary-adrenocortical axis and the sympathetic system are both under the control of the cerebral cortex, this hemisphere is thus primarily involved in the survival functions that enable the organism to cope with stress.

Drawing on Bowlby's notion that the infant's "capacity to cope with stress" is associated with certain maternal behaviours

(1969: 344), the attachment or bonding relationship directly shapes the development of the infant's right-brain stress-coping systems that operate at unconscious levels.

The right cerebral cortex contributes to the development of mother-infant interactions and shapes the capacity for biological synchrony, the regulatory system of attachment. This biological synchrony provides the basis for the empathic perception of emotional states. The right brain (non-dominant hemisphere) stores not only the representation of visceral and somatic states, and of the bodyself, but also an internal model of the attachment or bonding relationship and affect-regulation strategies. Neuropsychological studies now also indicate that it is the right hemisphere, not the verbal-linguistic left hemisphere, that develops later, and is the site of autobiographical and bodyself memory, where our past experiences are stored (Fink et al. 1996).

I speculate that it is here that the repertoire of the mother's body language is stored–her gestures, facial expressions, touch, smell, and posture, which contribute to forming the infant's bodyself image and posture.

During the first few years of life the brain is most open to being influenced and during this time important connections are formed and reinforced. Early experiences can alter the biochemistry and structure of the brain. Insecure attachments therefore undermine the baby's nervous system. Inappropriate or disattuned parental responses disturb the baby's body natural rhythms. This is why early support is most beneficial.

In Chapter 8, I explain in greater detail why early support is most beneficial. My decision to work with and write about parents and infants was led by my strong belief in the effectiveness of early support. By detecting the first signs of emotional problems it is possible to treat or prevent a number of "psychosomatic" illnesses. In my view, prevention is better that cure.

As a baby's brain is being wired, and is thus very plastic, early support leads to better outcomes than years of treatment later in life. Therefore it is much shorter than later treatment. Improving the relationship between parents and their babies is much more cost effective than any adult therapeutic treatment.

Because early emotions are imprinted, effective early support helps store healthy emotional experiences. Change can occur from one week to another. In my work with parents and babies, I have witnessed lifeless babies who did not make eye contact, and who lacked physical energy, suddenly springing to life as the mother's psychosomatic difficulties were resolved, or she became attuned to her baby (she responded to her effectively). The baby becomes more alert, starts to make eye contact, smiles, and his or her motor behaviour thrives. The case illustrated in this book is a vivid example.

What enables babies to thrive is responsiveness and attunement. This means that parents need to respond to the actual needs and feelings of their individual babies, and not to their ideal babies. This is the essence of emotional/physiological regulation: responding to what is actually happening in the moment to their particular baby, and processing feelings with that baby. There is no guide for a parent on how to do that. It is important that parents be attuned to their needs in order to be able to connect with their babies" needs and respond adequately. By having their states recognised, babies can then acknowledge their own states and build "true" or "grounded" bodyselves.

I suggest that many forms of adult psychosomatic dysfunctions are rooted in infancy and in the way that babies learn to regulate themselves. When babies do not have a caregiver who responds to their actual needs, thus regulating their emotional states, they tend to regulate themselves, for instance, by building a second defensive skin. We can see defensive patterns of emotional regulation in the mother presented in this book.

The objective of psychotherapeutic work with parents and infants is to release emotional inhibition. Healthy emotional life is without blockages. Holding in feelings, which corresponds to held breath, does not enable the child to regulate feelings and leads to psychosomatic symptoms.

Good regulation is related to feelings that flow freely through the body and the mental capacity to acknowledge them and reflect upon them. Good regulation is therefore the foundation of what I call in my book *Mothers, Babies, and their Body Language* "integrated bodyself". When body, feelings, and mind work in harmony, emotions are never frightening, but are used as a guide to social behaviour. They are the roots of a true or grounded bodyself.

When the mother's bodyself image is integrated, such that mind and body are in harmony, the prenatal and post-natal baby occupies an equal space in her mind and in her body. This means that the developing baby needs to be sensed and thought about at the same time.

The development of the prefrontal cortex, nourished by a responsive caregiver–usually the parents–represents the higher social brain and is responsible for advanced social behaviour. In order to manage our feelings in response to others, we need to take into consideration others" feelings, which is the essence of empathy. When a mother is faced with psychosomatic difficulties, she is unable to accept her feelings and manage them well in relation to her baby. Through early work with parents and infants, we encourage the development of the prefrontal cortex, and thus of the child's higher social behaviour. In other words, we work for a better society.

Chapter 9 highlights the importance of infant observation in preparing for psychotherapeutic work with parents and infants. The experience of seeing the importance of mother-infant attunement, the infant's capacity to make his or her needs known through body language (such as small movements), of intense feelings aroused by the mother and infant, and of becoming able to contain them, and other significant aspects, will remain inside the observer, available for future work with parents and infants.

Having the opportunity to discuss the written observations in a small seminar group offers observers a space for containing the anxieties and other emotions aroused by the observations, and for thinking and reflection. Listening to the thoughts of colleagues on the mothers and infants they have been observing enables each observer to understand the diversity and uniqueness of each mother-infant relationship. This leads to a less judgemental attitude in clinical work, which is fundamental to genuinely listening and connecting with the parent and infant.

I place an emphasis on some aspects of the infant observation experience that are familiar to Eastern approaches in psychotherapeutic work and the healing relationship. Working with parents and infants provides an opportunity to develop an integrative approach to the psyche-soma, which recognises the importance of this work as a whole. Effective therapeutic work relies on an integrative approach, simply because the human being functions as a whole, in which all the parts are woven together inseparably. We can clearly see this in an infant–for instance each tiny movement is an expression of needs, feelings, or states–and we cannot separate any form of body language from the manifestations of the psyche.

Observation is the foundation of research, theory, and clinical practice. Any professional concerned about parents and infants would benefit enormously from observational skills and from the emotional impact that the infant observation experience can have on them. The capacity to observe and to get to know your emotions can only develop through experience. In this chapter I will emphasise the importance of the clinician's capacity to face her/his feelings in order to be able to "empathise" with the client (in this case with a parent and infant), and thus to connect with their difficulties. This aspect is the basis of effective work with parents and infants. In this respect, infant observation can be an invaluable training not only for psychotherapeutic work, but also for many other professions.

In Chapter 10, I finally propose some principles upon which a "home" for clinical work with parents and infants and for infant observation settings should be built. The concept of the beneficial function of psychosomatic symptoms, such as mastitis, is central to the development of such a home. A psychosomatic symptom is crucial in its ability to communicate (to the therapist as well as to the patient) the need for change as well as the path through which it may occur. It informs of a split between psyche and soma.

Early experiences of body movements, touch, and of maternal holding are stored in the body. They impact on the development of a grounded bodyself and of an integrated psyche-soma. I assume that in adult life they mould the way a mother uses her body in interacting with her baby. Inadequate experiences of handling and loving are here seen as altering the unity of the psyche-soma–body and self are split–and the body is experienced as an object rather than as the venue of the self. This results in psychosomatic symptoms.

I highlight the active contribution of the infant to psychotherapeutic work with parents and infants and the infant's extraordinary capacity for recovery, thanks to her/his remarkable brain plasticity and behavioural flexibility.

I suggest that infant massage has the potential to be an integral part of psychotherapeutic work with parents and infants, when the physical experience is linked to "memories-in-feelings" (Klein 1957: 180) and can be elaborated in terms of object relations. The baby massage teacher has the potential to offer a "reflective space" by her containing function, which gives significance to infant massage and highlights the difference between mindful and mindless massage.

I suggest that infant-parent psychotherapeutic work, especially in the case of psychosomatic symptoms in the parent-infant dyad, should not remain the exclusive territory of psychotherapists. Collaboration with staff of a general practice or a baby clinic may be of the utmost importance. Midwives and health professionals working with parents and infants should be trained to acknowledge the emotional aspects of breastfeeding problems and to develop an integrated approach to psychosomatic problems. Experienced practitioners with parents and infants from different professional backgrounds can be enabled to enrich their work with the additional understanding that infant-parent psychotherapy brings, and with the experience of infant observation.

CHAPTER 1

A historical examination of the psyche-soma

In this Chapter I explore some theoretical gaps and imbalances in the psychoanalysis of the psyche-soma. The philosophy of dualism owes much to Christian theology. Descartes (1644) regarded mind and body as two separate entities, composed of different substances and governed by different laws. He deemed that the body, being a material object, could be explored via scientific investigation but that the mind could only be investigated via introspection. Since then, Western philosophers have struggled with the mind/body dilemma for over 300 years. This has profoundly affected the evolution of thinking in the field of psychoanalysis about the psyche-soma.

Psychoanalysis has been involved with the psyche-soma from the very beginning, when Freud began to treat patients with the physical symptoms of conversion hysteria via a "talking cure" (Freud and Breuer, 1893). For Freud a difficult task for the individual resided in controlling physically-based sexual drives seeking immediate gratification, and adapting them to the "reality principle" of social expectations (1911b). Although Freud described the ego as a "body ego', he substantially deemed mental and bodily functions to be opposed rather than complementary.

The complexity of mind/body entanglement as described in Freud's cases shows how a simple cause/effect relationship between mind and body is not appropriate. This is clearly confirmed in his notion of over-determination of symptoms (1901), which is widely accepted within psychoanalysis. Psychoanalysis does acknowledge that a delineation drawn by medicine between the psychological or somatic nature of certain illnesses is not possible and that it represents an oversimplification.

McDougall has described the "early pre-speech" infant's state; the infant depends upon the body for self-expression. In her book *Theatres of the Body* (McDougall, 1989, p. 87), she considers an adult patient's psychosomatic disorder to be "an attempt to take flight from intolerable affective states of anger and abandonment that she could neither contain nor elaborate." McDougall has explained that because emotions are psychosomatic, the incapacity to be in touch with a child's emotional needs may lead a child to develop the symptoms as a defence against emotional suffering.

McDougall's work has made substantial contributions to the understanding of psychosomatic processes through psychoanalysis. Her valuable ideas allowed many psychotherapists to reach an understanding of somatic manifestations. Yet, in spite of the major contributions it has made to our understanding, McDougall's work remains essentially dualistic. She has stated (1974, p. 441): "At this point we come back to the fact that the mental and the physical are indissolubly linked yet at the same time essentially different." McDougall struggled with the same dilemma that has concerned philosophers for hundreds of years. She acknowledged that the psyche-soma "functions as an entity', yet she also wrote (1974, p. 443): "Nevertheless, theoretical confusion will result if we overlook the fact that somatic processes and psychic processes are governed by different laws of functioning.'

Dualism has created, rather than resolved theoretical confusion. In the area of psychoanalytic infant observation, for example, the psyche-soma is conceived as one indivisible entity:

> The physical sensations and experiences of a baby are seen as part of a unified continuum of physical and mental states. The significance for observers of a baby's sense of physical togetherness, or panic, or

attachment through sucking (or biting) to the mother, is that it is expressive
of a baby's whole state of mind/body, not a physical action alone. [Rustin
1989: p. 62].

Klein (1935, 1946, 1948) retained the Freudian notions of instincts
and physical drives but propounded that these drives emerged
only in a context of relationship to another object, whether real or
a phantasy. She was interested in observing and listening to small
children while playing. Whilst Kleinian theory did not address the
mind/body dilemma, their implicit continuity emerges in Klein's
clinical work on disturbed children, where she saw the emotional
and physical aspects of an idea's elaboration and expression. For
example, with regard to phantasies, Isaacs (1948, p. 112) wrote
that: "The earliest phantasies are experienced in sensations; later
they take the form of plastic images and dramatic representations.
Phantasies have both psychic and bodily effects, e.g. in conversion
symptoms, bodily qualities, character and personality, neurotic
symptoms, inhibitions and sublimations.'

Winnicott was originally a Kleinian but later he developed his
own ideas. Winnicott's view of the psyche-soma and its effects on
other key concerns has attracted my attention. His focus on health,
on normal development, and on the positive function of a symptom
illuminates my therapeutic work.

While psychoanalysis operated within a dualistic framework of
mind and body as "composed of different substances" (Descartes
1644), Winnicott adopted a phenomenological framework based
on Heidegger's (1927) idea of physical "in-dwelling', described
by Winnicott (1962b, p. 68) as: "The achievement of a close and
easy relationship between the psyche and the body, and body
functioning."

Initiated by Hegel (1807) and elaborated by Heidegger (1927),
phenomenology emphasised description and observation, which
is what was central to Winnicott's experience. For Winnicott any
separation between psyche and soma resided in the onlooker, in the
choice of perspective rather than within the subject himself. This
idea is conveyed in the following passage:

Here is a body, and the psyche and the soma are not to be distinguished
except according to the direction from which one is looking. One can

look at the developing body or the developing psyche. I suppose the word psyche here means the imaginative elaboration of somatic parts, feelings and functions, that is, of physical aliveness. [Winnicott 1949, p. 244]

Phenomenological perspectives have recently influenced psychoanalytic thinking. These have made important contributions to the mind/body dilemma. In her paper on Sandor Ferenczi and his influence on Melanie Klein, Likierman argued for the impossibility of separating mental and physical aspects of functioning, even within the "talking cure" of psychoanalysis:

By implication, psychoanalytic interpretation, like all verbal expressions, cannot escape intimate links with the body. It is inseparable from sounds that are emitted physically, and thus from intonation, volume, rhythm and other forms of primitive enactment. Such an "active" element is not necessarily a disadvantage, for it gives transference interpretations an unconscious vitality that constitutes their communicable value. [Likierman 1993: 446]

With hermeneutics (Rustin, 1991) the emphasis shifted from the cause and aetiology to the meaning. Attention was now drawn to the meaning of a psychosomatic symptom, on what it is communicating, and to the individual's subjective experience.

Winnicott argued that verbal self-expression stands alongside, rather than replaces, self-expression via the body. On a similar line of thought, Turp has written:

In many instances "showings" may healthily take up a place alongside "telling', offering alternative paths for self-expression with a particular eloquence of their own. From this perspective, we can perhaps view sport or dance or yoga with less suspicion, regarding the body, rather in the way we regard dreams, as a potentially creative site of symbolisation, elaboration and self-expression. [Turp 1998, p. 12]

In my book *Mothers, Babies and their Body Language,* I argue for the inseparability of body and mental functions:

Our body is involved in our relationships as much as our mind. The two levels of our being are inseparable and a circular relation exists between them. They are split only by language and concepts. While thinking, speaking, dreaming, and interacting, there are changes in our breathing, muscle tone, posture, and facial expression–throughout our body language. They are powerful forms of non-verbal communication. [Sansone, 2004, p. 51]

In Winnicott's 1949 paper, "The mind and its relation to the psyche-soma', he used the term "psyche" to refers to "that part of the body capable of mental functioning" (1949, p. 95). The term "mind" refers to what we would describe as thinking. For Winnicott health in the individual's early development entailed "continuity of being'. For the healthy development of the early psyche-soma there is a need for a perfect environment, which actively adapts to the needs of the early psyche-soma. The mind/thinking splits off from the psyche-soma when a severe environmental failure "disturbs the continuity of being'. Then "excessive mental functioning" substitutes the function of the maternal care.

Winnicott wrote (1949, p. 243): "I venture to predict that the antithesis which has baffled all the philosophers will be found to be based on an illusion. In other words, I do not think that the mind exists as an entity–possibly a startling thing for a psychologist to say." In the following quote he condensed his own ideas on the mind/body (1949, p. 244): "The mind does not exist as an entity in the individual's scheme of things provided the individual psyche-soma or body schemes have come satisfactorily through the very early developmental states; mind is then no more than a special case of the functioning of the psyche-soma."

A central idea in Winnicott's thinking was that any separation of psyche and soma is a sign of disturbance. Over the course of his work, he increasingly put forward the importance of experienced "in-dwelling" (1962b) as a basis for continuity of being–a basis for feeling real. The foundations of this experience reside in maternal handling and holding, which is later accompanied by thinking and language.

On the same line of thought about mind/body, an observational study of mother-baby interaction (Sansone, 2002) suggested to me that an infant's posture, breathing, and body language in general begin to organize in relation to the primary caregiver's body language. An entire world of emotional/physical vibrations condition the baby's muscular tone and internal world, as well as those of the caregiver, and sow the seeds of health. There is no boundary between the emotional and the muscular, or general physical, levels.

> At first, the baby responds to the physical stimulation of the mother's hands: as the mother touches her, the baby adjusts her position and the mother then accommodates her gestures to the child's position. Bodily signals are transmitted from one to another. The quality of touch induces a feeling and modulates the child's postural response. The child thus has a complete experience. An interchange of muscular tone information gives rise to mutual postural adjustments. Physical or emotional tension weakens the capacities of mother and infant to rhythmic adjustments, making mutual understanding difficult. [Sansone, 2004, p. 202]

In his 1949 paper, Winnicott deemed that in its beginning a good (psychological) environment is a physical one, with the child in the womb, being held and generally tended to; only in the course of time does the environment develop emotional, psychological, or social characteristics.

The value of Winnicott's observations about the importance of the early environment in shaping the psychological functioning has increasingly been acknowledged by new developments in the neurosciences. The functioning of the brain is conceived of in a new way and bridges between disciplines seem to being built. For example, with regard to neuroscience and its relevance to psychoanalytic thinking Olds and Cooper wrote (1997, p. 221): "Where once we were concerned about the reductionism of some forms of biology, today's biological forefront is based on hierarchical systems theory, recognising emergent properties, and is unconcerned with trying to reduce poetic understanding to neuronal activity."

Major neuroscientific researchers such as Damasio (1999) and LeDoux (1996) have contributed to integrating neuroscience with psychology and psychotherapy. Emotion cannot be reduced to a few simple elements, but involves facial and other motor system changes, physical and autonomic changes, cognitive processes, and subjective feelings.

In my book *Mothers, Babies and their Body Language*, I argued that emotion is a subjective process involving different levels–cellular, hormonal, nervous, muscular, and behavioural–holding the whole system together and reflecting fundamental adaptive integration (Sansone 2004). The psychological level is the most complex, as it is the result of an intricate interrelationship between all levels. For example, fear involves a neural circuit in the brain and a hormonal process such as adrenaline release, with its effect on pupil size, heart rate, breathing, body temperature, hairs, muscle tone, posture, and facial muscles (Ruggieri, 1987). The subjective feeling of fear is the result of all these changes.

Finally, I refer to the illuminating work of Turp (1998), who considers the contribution of bodily experience to emotional well-being. I share her adoption of the term "beneficial psychosomatic processes" and I apply it to baby massage, conceived here as an integral part of psychotherapy. I am suggesting that the contribution of baby massage to the mother-infant relationship is that of feeling whole, within a skin, and of opening windows to bodily "indwelled" experiences of early life. In particular, I refer to the significance of the containing function of the infant massage teacher. The activation of sensory channels of communication fostered by the practice of baby massage–touch, eye contact, movement, vocalization, and smell, accompanied by a space for projections and verbal self-expression–involves a coming together of action, thinking, and feeling that leads to psychosomatic integration.

A central idea in *Mothers, Babies and their Body Language* is that:

> Any activity, whether it is lifting an arm, or walking, talking, going to sleep, learning something, thinking out a problem, or making a decision, involves an interrelationship between "mental" and "physical" processes and it is impossible to separate activities into either purely mental or purely physical. The distinction between "mental" and "physical" is merely a construct based on a particular observational perspective. [Sansone 2004, p. 7]

I call this unity of mind and body "psychophysical integration', which is the foundation of health. Disharmony between mind and body is a sign of disturbance. An example is when excessive emotional tension manifests itself through the mother's tightened gesture while breastfeeding, in muscular tension while holding her baby, in her sharp tone of voice, or her inability to verbalize her feelings and internal world.

Babies are particularly sensitive to the close relationship between the mental and physical states of their caregivers. They sense their emotional state through their muscular tension and movements. They will sense if they are being held confidently, nervously, lovingly, or rejectingly. By sensing the congruence between emotional states, muscular tone, and body language, babies can build psychosomatic integration. When the mother's mind and body live in harmony, she will be able to convey congruent messages through her body language, and through mirroring, so that her child will build an integrated and harmonious bodyself image.

CHAPTER 2

The psyche-soma within an object-relations framework

Winnicott put at the centre of his developmental model not a mythic conflict between incompatible forces but the localisation of self in one's body. For Winnicott, there was the body at the root of development out of which a "psychosomatic partnership" evolved. The self was first and foremost a body self and the "psyche" of the partnership meant the imaginative elaboration of somatic parts, feelings and functions, that is, of physical aliveness. (Phillips 1988, p. 78)

What I find particularly relevant was Winnicott's interest in distressing psychosomatic symptoms that he encountered in his psychoanalytic practice. Nevertheless, he was also interested in the relationship of psyche and soma in health and in normal development as well as in illness. Phillips (1988, p. 5) drew attention to Winnicott's questions: "What do we depend on to make us feel alive, or real? Where does our sense come from, when we have it, that our lives are worth living? Winnicott approached these issues through the observation–one of his favoured words–of mothers and infants, and what became in time the "transitional space" between them."

The blossoming of infant observation within psychoanalysis (e.g. Miller, Rustin, Rustin, & Shuttleworth, 1989) has provided new accounts of a "normal" infancy.

In his book *Clinical Notes on Disorders of Childhood* (1931), Winnicott emphasised his interest in the relationship between psyche and soma, in health as well as in disturbance. He clearly saw "the localization of self in one's body" (Phillips 1988). He regarded the self in health as wholly bound up with bodily aliveness, while in illness as deprived of that personal spontaneity or aliveness.

In Winnicott's early book of 1931 his central concern was on the struggles of individual infants and adults in a life that is inherently difficult for every human being. He describes some symptoms common during infancy and childhood, for example, enuresis, eczema, or refusing food, not as pathological manifestations but as a normal part of a child's development, simply because life is challenging for everybody.

In his 1966 paper, Winnicott highlighted the positive function of somatic symptoms, as they represent an attempt to maintain in some form an altered psychosomatic relationship. This concept is central to this book. In the same paper, the infant's environment, represented by the mother and the way she responds physically and emotionally to the infant, became of utmost importance. Although Winnicott was originally a Kleinian, he later placed a major emphasis on the importance of the environment. Klein (e.g. 1946, 1948) took a major step forward in psychoanalysis by placing far more emphasis than Freud on the mother-infant relationship, yet she still saw it as the ground of inevitable psychic conflicts. The first relationship was also Winnicott's central focus, yet he moved away from Klein's emphasis on constitutional factors.

Winnicott (1962a) referred to three fundamental maternal functions: "holding", "handling", and "object-presenting". He condensed his concept of "personalisation" in the following passage:

> The ego is based on a body ego, but it is only when all goes well that the person of the baby starts to be linked with the body and the body functions, with the skin as a limiting membrane. I have used the term personalisation to describe this process, because the term depersonalisation seems at basis to mean a loss of firm union between ego and body, including id-drives and id-satisfaction. [1962a, p. 59]

Winnicott saw any precocious development of mental functioning as a consequence of a failure in mothering:

Certain kinds of failure on the part of the mother, especially erratic behaviour, produce over-activity of the mental functioning. Here, in the overgrowth of the mental functioning reactive to erratic mothering, we see that there can develop an opposition between mind and the psyche-soma...The thinking of the individual begins to take over and organize the caring for the psyche-soma, whereas in health it is the function of the environment to do this. [1949, p. 246]

Winnicott referred to the differentiation between inside and outside:

Gradually the psyche and the soma aspects of the growing person become involved in a process of mutual interrelation. The interrelation of the psyche with the soma constitutes an early phase of individual development. At a later stage the live body, with its limits, and with an inside and an outside is *felt by the individual* to form the core for the imaginative self. [1949, p. 244]

In similar vein, Bick (1968) described the physical and psychic function of the skin. She emphasised the fundamental importance of the skin as a means of communication between mother and infant where she provides the holding environment, in which primary identification of the self is rooted.

The central theme of this brief communication is concerned with the primal function of the skin of the baby and of its primal objects in relation to the most primitive binding together of parts of the personality not as yet differentiated from parts of the body...But this internal function of containing the parts of the self is dependent initially on the introjection of an external object experienced as capable of fulfilling this function. [Bick 1964, p. 114]

One of a baby's most primitive and fundamental needs is to find a caregiver to be held by. The sense of being held gives the baby security and establishes the foundation for his or her self-confidence. Bick describes how the physical experience of being held in the arms of the mother provides the infant with a sense of being held together inside a skin. Through her handling of the child, the mother's skin may convey a full range of emotions, from tenderness and warmth and love, to disgust and hate. The baby is born with integrative competence, but needs an intuitive caregiver to attune and resonate with her psychophysiological states to maintain an integrated psyche-soma (Papousek & Papousek, 1987).

I consider that the psychic skin is equated by the baby with the physical skin, and that the skin's experiences, through touch, affect the development of the baby's personality.

> The primary function of the skin is to contain. It functions as a boundary. Through the contact with the mother, the baby introjects the experience of being held, which strengthens her psychic and physical skin and her sense of security. This relates to a process called "projective identification." By introjecting a containing object (mother, breast, and all the physical/sensual experiences with her), the baby cements an internal space and identifies with that object and with the experience it provides. [Sansone, 2004, p. 72]

In her 1968 paper, Bick argued that the introjection of an external object might be experienced as capable of containing the parts of the self. Failure to introject the containing function and thus disturbed "primal skin" formation may result in the development of a "second skin'. This is tough and impermeable, capable of holding the infant together, but at the expense of a capacity for relationships. As a consequence, failure in maternal physical holding may be at the basis of an infant's relative lack of integration, disturbances of posture and movement, and excessive self-reliance.

If the mother is absent, either physically or emotionally, and thus unable to contain the baby's needs, the baby has to find ways of holding itself to survive. For instance, he or she can relate to the light and smile and coo at it. The light may be experienced by the baby as a substitute for the mother. He or she may engage in continuous bodily movements that can act as a containing skin.

A form of self-holding is tightening of the muscles, and clenching sets of muscles together in a rigid position. This mechanism can involve not only skeletal muscles but also the smooth muscles of the internal organs, so that a spasm might result, for example, in colic or constipation. If these defensive survival mechanisms persist because of the mother's inability to meet the baby's needs, for instance when she is tired or depressed, they may become part of the baby's personality and impinge on his or her psychosomatic integration. This also impinges on the development of harmonious posture, motility, and gestures, and on body language in general.

In a similar vein to Bick, I wrote in my book *Mothers, Babies and their Body Language* (Sansone, 2004, p. 73) that: "The perpetuation of these survival mechanisms, through a disturbance in the primary skin function, can lead to the development of a substitute skin, a tough and rough skin, a type of muscular shell, that can be identified within a rigid posture..." I explained that these survival mechanisms are substitutes for the containing mother.

Bick (1964, p. 115) wrote that: "Disturbance in the primal skin function can lead to a development of a "second-skin" formation through which dependence upon the object is replaced by a pseudo-independence, by the inappropriate use of certain mental functions, or perhaps innate talents, for the purpose of creating a substitute for this skin container function." This suggestion has implicit mind/body implications. Certain "mental functions" represent a "second skin', which is also a precocious development of the skin.

Winnicott argues that when the harmony of the psyche-soma is lost, the infant or adult does not experience the body as reliable and the sense of self is fragile. Normal development is made possible by the ordinary "good enough mother" with her ability to make active adaptation to her baby's needs. The infant is allowed to live in its body rather than to think too much, and to maintain psychosomatic integration.

Phillips (1988, p. 79) highlighted the importance given by Winnicott to maternal handling in fostering integration within the infant: "This natural tendency to integrate is made possible by the mother's care in which the infant is kept "warm, handled and bathed and rocked and named.'

Winnicott (1949) explained that it is a characteristic maternal function to provide "graduated failure of adaptation', according to the growing ability of the infant to compensate for failure via mental activity or understanding. Winnicott made it clear that the timing of the process is important, which is specific to each individual mother-infant relationship, and the mental function must not develop so precociously as to disturb the infant's sense of "continuity of being'.

Similarities emerge between Winnicott and Bion, for example between Winnicott's concept of "holding" (1960a, 1960b) and Bion's concept of "containment" (1962b). They both describe periodic feeding as a communication between mother and baby based on a rhythmical exchange of cues, in which the infant's need to be fed and comforted are both met. This encounter is strongly dependent on the mother's perception of her psychobiological synchrony and its symbiotic bond with the baby's needs. This requires the mother to be able to feel and trust her body and focus on what is going on (Sansone 2004, p. 240).

Winnicott argued that the mother's milk does not flow like an excretion. It is a response to a variety of elements: the sight, smell, feeling, and thinking of the baby. Bion (1962b) refers to a "thinking breast'.

Bion offered more detailed descriptions of maternal reverie and of the mother's capacity to think about the baby's needs and experiences and to return them to the baby in a manageable form. In doing so, the mother gives the infant time to experience and develop thinking. However, it is Winnicott's work that provides lucid descriptions of mother-infant communication in terms of mutual physical experience. He wrote (1988) of "quiet yet live holding" and "rocking", which "ensures against depersonalization or loss of the psychosoma partnership". In *Mothers, Babies and their Body Language*, I wrote of congruent holding/communication, which ensures against the loss of psychosomatic integration (Sansone 2004). I assume that this congruent holding while feeding sets the foundation of the child's nutritional behaviour.

Unlike Freudians and Kleinians, for Winnicott physicality was not equated with sexuality, but with identity. Bion's central focus was upon the development of thinking, considered problematic only when it is lacking or impaired. Winnicott, however, viewed too much thinking as a sign of a divorce between psyche and soma and thus a sign of disturbance. In his descriptions of the maternal containing function, Bion referred to the body in terms of metaphors, while Winnicott was interested in the experiences of the body as well as in mental activities and in their partnership.

Bion's and Winnicott's ideas have made complementary contributions to the field of infant observation. Bion's accounts of maternal reverie and of the infant's internalization of the mother's capacity to think, and Winnicott's emphasis on the importance of physical handling have been of great value to theoretical constructs arising from infant observation.

In "Mind and its relation to the psyche-soma" (1949), Winnicott presented a clinical illustration of mental functioning that took over to replace the unreliable mother. This led to what Winnicott called "a false personal growth on a compliance basis", an issue that he fully developed in his paper "Ego distortion in terms of true and false self" (1960a).

Winnicott (1949, p. 250) described a 47-year-old female patient, whose central issue was a feeling of being "unreal', of living an "as if" life devoid of meaning or authenticity: 'The patient's whole life had been built around mental functioning which had become falsely the place (in her head) from which she lived, and in her life, which had rightly seemed to her false, had been developed out of this mental functioning.'

Winnicott enabled the patient to regress to a prenatal stage. She relived the birth process many times and each time she re-experienced a new aspect of it, such as breathing changes and feelings of constriction along her body. The regression culminated in terrible feelings of pressure on the head and the terrifying release of pressure that followed. Winnicott wrote:

> There had to be a temporary phase in which the breathing of her body was all. In this way the patient became able to accept the not-knowing condition because I was holding her and keeping continuity by my own breathing, while she let go, gave in, knew nothing... Now for the first time she was able to have a psyche, an entity of her own, a body that breathes and in addition the beginning of fantasy belonging to the breathing and other physiological functions. (Winnicott 1949, p. 252)

Having re-experienced the birth process, the patient could feel life as a "a real individual who feels real'. In this clinical case, it is clear that feeling real is intrinsic to feeling embodied, to a sense of self that is experienced not as localized in the head but rather as throughout the entire body. It is also clear that the analytical setting recreates in some form the primal maternal holding–"*I was holding her and keeping a continuity by my own breathing.*" He was recreating in a different form intimacy with the first object. Winnicott was not rigidly opposed to limited physical contact in the psychoanalytical setting. He underpinned the physical facilitation of the patient's regression and restaging of events.

In his 1953 paper "Transitional objects and transitional phenomena', Winnicott described these interrelated concepts in their concrete physicality. He referred to an intermediate area of experiencing, formed by both inner reality and external life (1953, p. 230): "It is an area which is not challenged, because no claim is made on its behalf except as it exists as a resting place for the individual engaged in the perpetual human task of keeping inner and outer reality separate yet interrelated."

Transitional objects allow the infant to hold and soothe him or herself and to manage excessive anxiety and total dependency upon his mother. By holding and touching them the child can tolerate separation or physical hurt. Transitional objects are both *mental*, as they occupy a space in the psyche, and *physical*, as the child is involved in a relationship to them with the whole of his or her body–the way of holding, touching, cuddling, and carrying them. I suggest that the practice of baby massage may make important contributions to the infant's transitional area. It may also bring to recall, through touch, massage movements, the infant's vocalization and live movements in response to being massaged, the quality of the mother's own transitional objects and experiences.

In her book *A Woman's Unconscious Use of her Body* (1993), Pines examined the ways in which the mind expresses itself through a woman's body, and conversely, the manner in which the body's experiences impinge upon the mind. Particularly relevant to this book is her view of mothering as an embodied three-generational experience. There is a psychic reality, based on the mother-infant relationship that has been experienced by the future mother, which may be conflicting and in its turn determines the future of the mothering in these cases. On a physical level the problem is posed as to whether the pregnant woman is to identify herself with her introjected mother or to rival her and succeed in being a better mother than she was felt to have been.

In *Mothers, Babies and their Body Language* (Sansone, 2004), I explain that primary feelings are stored in our muscle memory and shape our posture, breathing activity, bodyself image, and body language, as do other factors that are genetic and cultural, as well as the physical environment (e.g. diet, childhood illness, and injuries).

All these elements affect the quality of parenting.

Later I wrote:

> Major life experiences such as pregnancy and parenthood raise unresolved issues related to our earliest experiences. A parent who was not handled sensitively as a baby, so that her muscles did not store loving sensations and experiences, is more likely to repeat what she received, as posture and body language are programmed to reproduce what was stored in earliest memories. The way in which someone was cared for affects their bodyself perception and image. Although later experience will be incorporated into past relationships, it cannot undo established patterns, only modify them over time. [Sansone, 2004, p. 13]

The belief that parenting patterns are passed on may be well founded. Many studies have revealed that the way in which we were cared for and nurtured as infants and children affects how we parent, as well as how we interact with other people in general (Klaus, Kennell, & Klaus 1996). The perinatal, pregnancy, and post-partum periods can make early experiences resurface unexpectedly, without the parents being able to recognise their source or their effect on how to monitor their bodyself.

Pines wrote that unresolved conflicts and fantasies may involve both positive and negative representations of the self, and a continuation of ambivalent relationships with the parents and siblings of early childhood. An important factor in this is the "defensive splitting" and bypassing of the mental process through the use of the body. The mother creates with her thoughts and fantasies the physical (and psychological) environment of the foetus. As Pines stated (1993, p. 115) "The foetus inside her body represents good and bad aspects of the self and of the object (mother), and the mother may not give him a licence to live if she herself feels that she has never been granted one by her own mother."

I wrote (Sansone, 2004) that the mother-baby relationship is shaped during prenatal life and is exquisitely bodily, as the mother's inside world expresses itself through her body. I consider the mother's body the visible metaphor for her feelings about pregnancy, birth, and her baby.

Her bodyself image is a psychophysical process that continuously adjusts to the emotional and physical change brought about by pregnancy, birth, and child-care. The way in which a woman perceives her bodyself seems to impinge on how the baby is fed, held, nurtured, and loved.

I explained that (Sansone, 2004, p. 18): "The mother's internal world, the meanings she gives to her baby's movements and signals, contribute to forming the uterine environment, thus the baby's core personality, in the same way as her hormones and biorhythms do...the pregnant woman creates the intra-uterine ambience with her feelings, breathing, attitudes to her bodyself, and motivation towards birth." For instance, if the mother is stressed, and breathing speeds up, the baby reacts accordingly. If this becomes a habitual pattern, the baby's respiratory activity and posture can be affected, as can her emotional life.

Pines wrote (1993, p. 120-121): "It is possible that the pregnant woman's unconscious anxieties connected with the fantasy of the foetus, representing a bad and dangerous aspect of the self or of her partner may be a contributing factor to the stimulation of uterine expulsive movements, which end in miscarriage." She commented that women who miscarry or consciously abort a foetus may have unconsciously somatized their childhood emotional difficulties by using their bodies to avoid conscious affects and fantasies that felt overwhelming to the young child's ego. By way of contrast, a mother's positive bodyself provides a happy environment for the foetus and helps with birth. Piontelli (1992) considered that a warm and softly pulsating uterus and pelvis is shaped by the mother's positive feelings and acts as an emotional container to provide the best environment and birth for the foetus.

Pines deemed that the task a woman has to accomplish in pregnancy and motherhood is to "integrate" reality with unconscious fantasies, hopes, and daydreams. She has, in addition, for the first time to meet the demands of a dependent creature that represents strongly cathected areas of self and non-self and many past conflicting relationships. She emphasised that the foundation of the self and the distinction between self and object are shaped by an integration of bodily experience with mental representation (1993). In Winnicott's terms, the future mother's capacity to integrate the regressive feelings brought on by pregnancy with adult reality is associated with the condition of "feeling real" (1949). This condition, which allows good access to emotional states and influences the outcome of pregnancy, is rooted in the experience of a "psyche-soma" that lives and works in harmony with itself (1967, p. 29).

I deem that the woman's attitude to her bodyself plays a major role in pregnancy. To be able to sense and understand the baby's rhythms and attune with him or her, the mother needs to be connected with her "integrated" bodyself and know its rhythm (Sansone 2002). An inner ideal child nurtured during pregnancy may be related to a failure in the integration of bodily experiences with mental activities (bodyself integration), which prevents a woman from accepting and connecting with the real baby.

In particular I want to turn to the subject of the positive function of somatic disturbance, which Winnicott described in his 1966 paper "Psycho-somatic illness in its positive and negative aspects." It is linked to the subject of the inseparability of psyche and soma and is a central theme. He stated (1949, p. 254) "In these terms we can see that one of the aims of psychosomatic illness is to draw the psyche from the mind back to the original intimate association with the soma."

Winnicott (1966) described a psychosomatic symptom as a sign of the dysfunction of the link between psyche and soma, whereas in health the tendency is towards integration and personalization, when a functioning personality develops within and harmoniously with a functioning body.

Winnicott's work, particularly in relation to psychosomatic integration and health and to the positive function of symptoms, illuminates my research and clinical work as well as my work as a baby massage practitioner. In this book I have drawn upon Winnicott's ideas in relation to the psyche-soma, relevant literature, child development research, developments in the area of touch physiology, and one clinical case from my work experience.

CHAPTER 3

The "bodyself" in early relationship

Research and clinical literature has paid very little attention to how a woman's bodyself may impinge on her parental skills and on the quality of her interaction with her baby, which is what gave me the idea to write my first book *Mothers, Babies, and their Body Language* (Sansone, 2004) and this chapter. In my first book, the relation between the woman's bodyself and her parenting abilities is extensively considered for the first time. Consideration is also given to how the mother's attitude to her bodyself can affect the development of the infant's bodyself. To nurture an integrated bodyself image and grow in self-confidence, a child needs a mother who values herself and has a fulfilled relationship with her body and self. A sense of guilt, hatred of life, or fear sends signals about self-esteem and about the importance of motherhood. Parents teach their child assertiveness and self-trust through their confident posture and firm way of holding, as their attitudes and feelings constantly take shape through their muscular tension and body language.

This book contains a chapter on the *bodyself* because I suggest that effective emotional support in pregnancy, birth, and child-care offered by psychotherapeutic work with parents and infants has to be aimed at leading a woman to get in touch with her bodyself, as the baby is dwelling in her body and needs a space in her mind as well. I believe that any deep therapy that acts on a mental level and ignores the active role played by the body leads a woman far away from a true connection with her baby. A parent communicates with her prenatal and newborn baby through bodily cues such as breathing, touch, eye contact, movement, and facial expression. Early support for parents and infants thus has to value these channels of communication.

I shall adopt the term "Bow Method" for an approach aimed at increasing sensory and bodily awareness and thus enhancing the sense of self. It focuses on rhythmic interactions and communication between parents and infant and between therapist, parents, and infants. What happens between mother and baby is represented here by the relationship between a musician and her instrument. Her talent is maximized when the instrument's strings are tuned in order to produce the right notes. In a similar way, the mother needs to play her own bodyself and body language to tune them to the prenatal and post-natal baby. Neither parent nor baby is either just the instrument or the musician. They alternately play each other, as their interactions are two-way. A baby's capacity to respond and interact with its mother may inspire all her mothering capacities. Alternatively, there are babies who are so dissatisfied from birth that they evoke in their mothers all their infantile anxieties and insecurities. For instance, the baby's cry can evoke primitive infantile fears in the parent or trigger projections associated with a negative meaning of crying, which do not relate to the baby's actual needs. These babies may be attacked, rejected, or ignored if their parents are not in contact with those anxieties and, unaware of them, carry on projecting them on to their child. On the other hand, there are mothers who are strong and confident enough or who receive enough support to be able to keep coping and make an adjustment.

When the mother's integrated bodyself and her associated self-confidence enable her to receive and contain the baby's fears, crying, and anger, giving her back these feelings in a renewed light rather than rejecting them, she allows her baby to acknowledge them through a mirroring process. If this process does not take place, the infant may escape from the frightening feelings and become unable to monitor them in later life. When the mother produces resistance, which hinders her from connecting with her emotions and inner child, her baby will have difficulty receiving back her own feelings and thus developing an integrated bodyself based on a true experience of self. Earlier on, I wrote that the child's integrated psyche-soma derives from a true experience of his or her bodyself.

What is "bodyself" image?

The distinction between "mental" and "physical" is merely a construct based on a particular observational perspective. In fact, any activity, whether it is lifting an arm, or walking, talking, sleeping, learning, or thinking out a problem, involves an interrelationship between "mental" and "physical" processes and it is impossible to separate activities into either purely mental or purely physical.

I call this unity of mind and body "psychophysical integration', which is one of the fundamental components of health. Psychotherapeutic work with parents and infants should therefore promote psychosomatic integration in the parent and consequently in the infant, to which bodyself integration is related. We experience the relationship between the mental and physical in our everyday lives. One example is the way in which anxiety can cause breathing difficulties, nausea, and stiff, jerky movements. Another example is the way in which we hold our breath when we are concentrating in order to solve a complicated mathematical problem. When we are afraid, we contract our facial muscles, producing a typical expression of fear.

To understand how the bodyself develops very early in life, it is worth knowing how body image develops. A body image is the result of two activities:

(1) The synthesis of sensory signals travelling from the body to the brain to produce a mental representation of the body's parts and activities.

(2) The monitoring of the body's activities to maintain a correspondence between a mental image and bodily attitudes.

There is a constant interrelationship between the two processes. In other words, a body image acts as a bridge between input–information from the body and its sensory channels (hearing, sight, smell, touch, taste, movements) to the brain–and output, i.e. mental control of the muscular activity in the postural attitudes.

Body image plays a fundamental role in modulating the relationship between posture, movement, and gesture, allowing the whole body to move in space. Posture is an integrated response to a variety of internal and external stimuli in the social and physical environment. It is the result of mechanical, emotional, and social factors. On the other hand, an individual's posture acts as a stimulus that can cause feelings of comfort/discomfort, confidence/insecurity, and stability/instability. For example, an individual shows "avoidance" behaviour through a backward posture, as tension pulls the body backwards. In a very different situation, an individual may show "approach" behaviour with open shoulders and chest, and a "forward" posture.

Body image is therefore the way in which an individual organizes muscular tension and uses the body and posture in accordance with mental states and attitudes. Our attitude to our body reflects the way in which we think and feel. The way in which we view ourselves is reflected in everything we do–how we breathe, talk, eat, walk, sit, and stand up. It reflects the way in which we organize our self and body perception, our posture, or our bodyself image.

Babies are particularly sensitive to the close relationship between the mental and physical states of their caregivers. They sense their emotional state through their muscular tension and movements. They will sense if they are being held confidently, nervously, lovingly, or rejectingly. Babies who are held in a confident, gentle, and sensitive manner will feel more secure and will learn to trust their parents.

A common complaint among mothers is strong tension in the upper arms, shoulders, and neck. This is often aggravated by unskillfully holding the baby. An effective use of the arms that can provide a fulfilling experience of containment requires an effective use of the bodyself. The amount of tension that a mother may have in her whole body directly affects the sensitivity that she has in her hands, thus the quality of her touch. This is why early parent-infant support should take into consideration the way parents use their bodily expressions and their relationship to their emotions in the ongoing interactions with their babies.

The parent's body image therefore displays itself through her/his movements, posture, gestures, and facial expressions and affects the development of the baby's sense of body and self. This relationship begins very early in intra-uterine life. When a baby is in the womb, many of its actions and rhythms are synchronized with those of the mother. Maternal and infant behaviours complement each other in several sensory and motor systems, thus increasing the probability of interaction. They interact as a single system, although this is subject to environmental influences.

A baby picks up on its mother's attitude to her bodyself through her kinaesthetic sense and unconsciously learns to incorporate this into its behaviour. Our muscular memory is very powerful in early life. If a baby experiences fear, anger, or distrust too often, his or her muscular activity and posture will be affected and these emotions will be stored in muscle memory. The muscular system is a wonderful resource, enabling us to move, breathe, reach out, embrace, and kiss, thus to express our feelings through gestures, facial expressions, etc, and get in touch with our surroundings.

There is no psychological or relational process in which the body is not involved. The mind plays a major role in whatever we are doing and a healthy, well-functioning mind can make effective use of information from the body and display itself via the body in a feedback relationship. We certainly could not express a loving gesture, such as a kiss or hug, without the muscles that enable us to produce it. Any emotion displays itself through the interplay of facial muscles that picture a certain expression. And if the muscles involved in these gestures or in the facial expressions have excessive tension, the message cannot be communicated clearly.

Psychotherapeutic work with parents and infants has to look at the way parents organize their muscular tension in communicating their emotions to their babies through gestures, facial expression, tone of voice, and other forms of body language.

In *Mothers, Babies and their Body Language* (Sansone, 2004, p. 102) I wrote: "A gesture is a psychophysiological pattern that involves our muscular activity, emotional life, and belief system. When restrained by excessive muscle tension, a gesture can reflect inhibited emotion. In the long term, this phenomenon affects our well-being in the same way that a part of the body does when it stops functioning properly."

To restore a fragmented gesture, a psychotherapist will find it very helpful to bear in mind the close relationship between the different levels of functioning. There are still many physiotherapists who believe the cause of back pain, for instance, to be necessarily localized in the back. They therefore manipulate this area and do not even consider that a different area or an emotional disturbance might be involved.

The communicative function of a gesture also has to be considered, as it is a powerful cue in the repertoire of body language. Freeing a gesture from its inhibiting source, both at the emotional and at the muscular level, means enriched and effective communication, smoother posture, and a larger repertoire of movements and expressions. It often creates a feeling of fulfilled internal space that allows for a richer perception of the external social and physical environment.

These considerations, which concern human beings of all ages at all levels of well-being–physical, emotional, behavioural, relational, and communicative–point to the importance of unconstricted caring gestures from a parent while interacting with the developing infant. The baby senses the emotional content of the parent's gesture, facial expression, or tone of voice, when they are free from tension. The infant's gestural language is shaped by the way in which parents deal with their body language in the course of their interactions with him or her.

Any gesture or movement evolves through a balanced interplay of all parts of the body. While some muscles contract, others relax during a movement. For a gesture to evolve smoothly, everything needs to happen in harmony. The same occurs with facial expressions. However, if a muscle or group of muscles is in prolonged contraction rather than contracting and relaxing alternately, the evolution of the movement, gesture, or expression is constricted. Excessive tension prevents muscles from becoming relaxed. In clinical work, we often find emotional blockage to be responsible. Some individuals use held-back patterns as defensive adaptive mechanisms to repress feelings that they are unable to acknowledge. We will see these patterns in the mother presented in Chapter 5.

Smooth, balanced posture and movements require a rhythmic sequence of muscle contraction and relaxation. In most psychosomatic disturbances, these rhythmic patterns are altered. A prolonged muscle contraction (due to excessive tension) can be conceived as a "break point", a point that alters the natural evolution of a movement or gesture, its communicative function, and the perception of bodyself. We can change the way we use some parts of the body by acknowledging the emotional link. As a result, we can improve the general use of our body and self and experience a greater freedom of gesture. The sense of self will simultaneously change, as the use of our body is a reflection of our self and vice versa. Breathing will change as well, and the sensory channels open wide. The sensory channels are the windows that enhance our perception of our environment as well as of our body, and enrich our communication skills.

Visibly, some individuals use a very small percentage of their potential. They have grown so accustomed to their habitual uncomfortable posture that they are not aware of the multitude of mental and bodily strategies they use. Psychotherapeutic work has to be aimed at making parents aware of their muscular blockages and uncomfortable posture in order to develop free caring and loving gestures. Learning occurs together with feelings and dramatically involves the body and muscle memory. This is especially visible in the young baby, whose learning involves the whole body in a dramatic way. What we learn is recorded in our feelings and muscle memory and it manifests in our posture, gestures, and the way we deal with relationships. For example, a baby records the mother's voice not just by hearing it but also, and more importantly, by sensing the vibrations and rhythm of the sounds in her skin and muscles. He or she records its emotional quality. Together with her touch, eye contact, facial expression, and smell, the mother's voice modulates the baby's muscular and emotional activity, as well as other physiological activities such as respiratory, cardiac, and digestive functions, and by doing so she shapes the baby's posture and gestures.

The repertoire of the mother's body language, which contributes to forming the infant's bodyself image and posture, seems to be stored not just in the infant's brain but also in her body. The site of autobiographical and bodyself memory is not just the primal right brain (Fink et al, 1996, Schore, 1994; Schore, 2003b), but also the body with its muscular system, both the skeletal and visceral. The left hemisphere, which is the verbal-linguistic one, develops later and in relation to the right one. Emotional and muscular systems thus have a formative influence on verbal and cognitive development, in contrast to previous theories.

By acknowledging their own feelings and body language, a parent undertakes a journey through the exploration of the bodyself's creative potential, which is vital to establish an attuned relationship with his or her baby. This refers not only to parents but to all human beings. The primary muscle memory, where our earliest experiences are recorded, shapes the image of our bodyself and, likewise, the bodyself image affects our movements, posture, and body language. These processes in childhood have an impact that endures into our adult life, and thus cannot be understood in isolation from them.

During my work with the mother and baby presented in Chapter 5, I constantly focused on helping the mother acknowledge and understand her feelings and body language as valuable sources of creative potential to attune to her baby. I always paid attention to the drama played by her body, for instance, her tense gestures while breastfeeding, the symptom of mastitis, the "faraway" quality of her speech, and the lack of eye contact with me as well as with her baby. By doing so, the mother became increasingly aware of her body language and its emotional content and of her psychosomatic collision. The physical contact with her baby contributed enormously to this kind of liberating awareness.

I suggest that only by understanding the signs of their body-minds, the meanings of their psychosomatic symptoms, and their impact on their relationship to their babies, can parents truly understand the body cues, needs, and feelings of their babies and respond to them appropriately. Professionals working with parents and infants need to understand early signs of problems in babies and the signs of psychosomatic or bodyself disturbances in parents to allow for the baby's healthy development.

The mother-baby synchrony seems to be innate and instinctive, but in our industrialized society it has altered. This may be linked to a reduction of bodily contact and sensory communication between parents and babies–touch, eye contact, and attentive listening–that reduces the scope for getting to know each other through movements and bodily cues. It is often assumed that the mother will know instinctively how to handle a newborn baby but many women have never held one before and they feel tense and fearful. If they are in hospital, some women can feel intimidated by health professionals who are the "experts', and trust themselves even less.

A woman's attitude to her bodyself plays a major role in how she bonds with her baby. To be able to feel and understand the baby's needs and attune with him or her, the mother needs to be connected to her bodyself and know its rhythms. This will be highlighted in the mother-baby case illustrated in Chapter 5. The mother's acceptance of the baby is linked to her self-acceptance. Very often, the inner child nurtured during pregnancy prevents a woman from accepting and connecting with the real baby. Winnicott (1949) explained that the future mother's capacity to integrate the regressive feelings brought about by pregnancy with outer reality is associated with a psyche-soma that loves and works in harmony with itself.

It is an essential principle of attachment that parents must receive some responses or signals (such as bodily or eye movements) from their baby in order to form a close bond. This sensitivity to the baby's cues is directly affected by the amount of bodily tension that the mother has–the less tension there is and thus the more integrated her bodyself is, the more open are her sensory channels and thus the greater is her sensitivity. A woman in Africa who carries her baby on her back or side is regarded as a poor mother if her baby wets or soils itself, because this means that she has not anticipated this behaviour. This anticipation is based on bodily cues the baby gives.

This communication via body language is almost inconceivable in countries where mother and baby are kept apart much of the day and sleep separately at night. The primary movements and sensory communication help parents to become more quickly attuned to their baby and therefore to adapt their behaviour to his or her needs and pace. When sensory communication is hindered by the mother's concerns, as we can see in the case illustration in Chapter 5, the child's overall development can be altered, and psychosomatic illness is likely to develop. The rhythmic attuned communications have a self-regulatory function on the developing infant.

One observational study (Anisfeld, Casper, Nozyce, & Cunningham, 1990) compared a group of babies who were carried on the mother's body in a soft baby-carrier with another group that used firm infant seats that provided less contact. When the babies were three months old, the mothers using the soft baby-carriers were more responsive to their babies" cries and other signals. When all the babies were thirteen months old, the Ainsworth Strange Situation Test that measures attachment security was applied, with the finding that 83% of the babies carried on their mother's body in the soft carrier were securely attached, in contrast to only 39% of the babies from the group that used the firm baby seats (Ainsworth, Blehar, Waters & Wall, 1978). These findings suggest that early carrying (using soft baby-carriers) is a simple but effective way of establishing a healthy mother-infant relationship that affects the infant's future attachment and his or her physical and psychological development.

A mother's increased capacity to attune to her baby through physical contact can soften her habitual defences and bring her more in touch with her feelings. Close loving contact with the baby during breastfeeding can also be very pleasurable, sensual, and affirming. For some women, it can be the first time in their lives that they feel a complete self-acceptance, which can lead to a more integrated and fulfilling bodyself image. This demonstrates the wonderful power and ability of parents to change, grow, and modify attitudes and thus past experiences in relating to their babies. Child-care can bring added benefits if there is an awareness of the unity of self and body and of the role of the muscular system and posture in emotional and relational life. But if psychosomatic integration has been damaged by emotional deprivation in early life and thus the parent is concerned with emotional issues, she or he will not be able to meet and attune to the baby's needs.

A major goal of psychotherapeutic work with parents and infants has to be to increase integration of the bodyself and awareness of its importance in the parents, as it is passed directly on to the infant through mirroring, and is likely to manifest later on in the form of a balanced emotional life and posture and healthy overall development. If a mother has a healthy sense of her own body and self and is able to ensure that her own needs are met, she will be better able to love and care for her baby. Her movements in handling her baby and her loving gestures will be a reflection of her integrated bodyself.

Having a healthy sense of bodyself helps the mother to become aware of her boundaries–of where she and her baby begin, who she is, and who the other person is. This enables her to have a healthy sense of separateness from other people and from her baby, which is essential for closeness and bonding and thus for nurturing a deeper relationship with her baby. If the mother can learn to give herself the time and space for her own needs, her child will, through mirroring, learn the "otherness" of people, which is also fundamental in any healthy social interaction. However familiar a mother may be with babies, holding her baby is such an emotional experience that she may still feel a little anxious. Sometimes there are persistent fears that have not been resolved during pregnancy, as we can see in the case study in Chapter 5.

In the latter half of the pregnancy, both parents undergo a period of turmoil and self-questioning: "Will I ever get to be a parent? If I get to be a parent, will I have to be like my own parents?" Realizing that their only experience of parenthood was their own upbringing can make them afraid of failure in the new task. They ask themselves: "Have we made a mistake? Do we really want this baby?" Pregnancy, like any other major change, is a turning point in an individual's life. The acceptance of life change is closely related to the acceptance of bodily change, which allows the woman's bodyself image to fluctuate and adjust.

We may wonder why the turmoil arising in pregnancy is so universal and mobilizes all a parent's available emotional energy, especially during late pregnancy and after birth, sometimes turning into a period of depression. The ability to adjust and apply this energy to parenthood and bonding with the baby is essential. Where the turmoil persists after birth and parents are not supported, the bonding may be affected, since a parent's concerns and tension (acting through their bodies) can hinder the ability to sense the baby and get in touch with his or her needs.

I consider that this universal turmoil is linked to a process of rebirth, which mobilizes a parent's earliest experience of contact with their own parents. If a parent-to-be has lacked primary contact (they were not held properly, cuddled, touched securely, and so on), he or she is more likely to be overwhelmed by feelings of loss, grief, sorrow, anger, worry, and turmoil, which will affect bonding with the prenatal and newborn baby. The case illustrated in Chapter 5 will show the consequences of a parent's lack of primary contact in the parent-infant relationship, bonding, and the infant's well-being. As we have seen, Pines (1993) examined the ways in which the mind expresses itself through a woman's body and, conversely, how bodily experiences impinge on the mind. She viewed mothering as an embodied three-generational experience. Psychotherapeutic work with parents and infants has to consider the transgenerational experience of the parents, and if necessary, call on, in an analytic setting, the parents of the parents.

Our primary feelings are stored in our muscle memory and shape our posture, breathing activity, bodyself image, and body language, alongside other factors that are genetic, cultural, as well as the physical environment (e.g. diet, childhood illness, and injuries). Our bodyself can be seen as the psychophysical expression of a conglomeration of all aspects of life.

Major life events such as pregnancy and parenthood raise unresolved issues related to our earliest experiences. A mother who was not held sensitively as a baby, so that her muscles did not store warm sensations and loving experiences, is more likely to repeat what she received, in her posture and gestures, and in all the forms of body language that tend to reproduce what was stored in primal memory. The way in which someone was cared for affects their bodyself perception and image. Although later experience will be incorporated into past relationships, it cannot dissolve rooted patterns, but only modify them over time. This explains the extraordinary benefits of early support.

The belief that parenting patterns are passed on may be well founded. Many studies have revealed that the way in which we are cared for and nurtured as infants and children affects how we parent, as well as how we interact with other people in general (Klaus, Kennell, & Klaus, 1996). The perinatal, pregnancy, and post-natal periods make early experiences resurface unexpectedly, without the parents being able to recognize their source or their effect on how they monitor their bodyself.

Early care given to an infant is taken in via a complex mental and bodily process and affects her own parenting in later life. To give an example: Monica was born with a section of her oesophagus completely closed. She required feeding via a tube into her stomach and was never held in anyone's arms for feeding. At twenty-one months old, she had an operation–the passage was established and recovered. She was filmed over the next thirty years of her life and it was shown that in every feeding situation she repeated her own early feeding experience. She never held her doll in her arms as a little girl. Later, when she cared for her own four infants, she never held them in her arms. Her own experience in infancy became a model for her caregiving as a mother. This pattern may be carried into successive generations. Her four daughters held their dolls in a similar way to their mother.

The experience of touch with the baby may mobilize feelings such as anxiety, sorrow, and anger, and make a parent react with defence mechanisms and tightening of muscles. However, working through the contact with the baby in early support or psychotherapeutic work with parents and infants can be a crucial path to exorcising ghosts from the past. It consists in a working through in the context of the present relationship, through self-investigation and observation, rather than the distant past. Merely going back to the parents" primary experiences at such a delicate time as pregnancy and birth may increase the suffering and worry, and even drive parents away from their actual relationship with their baby, which consists mainly of bodily rhythmic interactions.

There are many opportunities for growth and renewal and it is a principal aim of effective support to make parents aware of these possibilities. The experience of touch with their baby makes parents and their overwhelming feelings related to early experiences more likely to turn into something positive. Bonding can repair the traumas they may have suffered as children. Early support can help both parents and babies experience the bond as a source of security and joy and as a pleasurable experience.

The kind of support based on the "contact experience", which enhances the parents" ability to respond and attune to their baby's needs, is vital in decreasing the risk of post-natal depression and other psychosomatic disturbances. As I will be discussing in Chapter 5, mindful baby massage, which promotes physical and emotional contact between parent and baby, can be an effective tool that can complement psychotherapeutic work with parents and infants.

CHAPTER 4

Touch, movement, and integration of the psyche-soma

> Part and parcel of holding is what Winnicott refers to as *handling*–the way the mother handles her infant in all the day-to-day details of maternal care. Here is included a mother's *enjoyment* of her baby, which is an expression of her love.
> (Abram, 1996, p. 187)

My primary focus here is on the early experiences of movement and touch, arising within the mother-infant relationship, described by Bick (1968) and Winnicott (1962b) as essential to the evolution of a sense of boundaries, a sense of skin, and a sense of bodyself.

The communication between mother and baby is triggered by a variety of channels: skin contact, smell, warmth, eye contact, interplay of facial expressions, vocalizing, movements–all sensual means, experienced by the infant as holding the parts of the personality together. All sensory experiences–sights, sounds, smells, etc.–have the potential to contribute to a sense of bodily aliveness, of feeling real (Winnicott, 1949). The sensory exchanges between mother and baby impinge on the infant's process of discovering her own being and boundaries. The mother's reproduction of the baby's facial expressions, sounds, and gestures encourages self-discovery even more than her stimulation and guidance (Sansone, 2004).

The skin is a medium for physical contact, for the comfort of holding and of being held, and also for the transmission of smell, touch, taste, and warmth, sensations that can be a source of pleasure and intimacy for both mother and infant alike (Pines, 1993). In accordance with Bick's work, Pines wrote that the skin, the most primitive channel for preverbal communication, establishes the boundary of the self and non-self, and represents the container of the self for each one of them. She has stated (1993, p. 9) that: "Through her handling of the child the mother may convey the full range of emotions, from tenderness and warmth and love to disgust and hate. The infant may respond through its skin to the mother's positive feelings by a sense of well being, and to her negative feelings by a skin disorder."

Movement is intimately related to touch. Movement involves not only muscular activity but also proprioception, which informs us of the position and speed of movement of parts of our body, and therefore has a quality of "inside touching".

I believe that there has been inadequate study of emotional bodily dynamics, or the way in which emotions "move". It seems no coincidence that the word "emotion" derives from "motion" or "movement'. The five channels of sensory communication–sight, touch, smell, hearing, and taste–have a sixth paramount aspect: movement and gesture. For instance, while a person is speaking, several parts of the body move in ways that can be either evident or fairly imperceptible. In the same way, the listener's movements can be coordinated with the speaker's rhythm of speech and bodily movements. When two people talking to each other are filmed, microanalysis reveals that both are moving in tune to the words being spoken, thus creating a type of dance in rhythm with the speech patterns. This phenomenon can appear quite clearly in the rhythmic conversation between mother and baby (proto-conversation).

A baby's skin is especially sensitive to touch. Through skin contact, a mother conveys non-verbal messages to her baby, who responds with changes in muscle tone, galvanic skin response, breathing, movements of the head, limbs, and of the whole body, eye contact, vocalizations, and sucking. These bodily interactions shape a rhythmic form of communication that is based on shared codes. These daily moments cement the relationship between parent and baby and will shape awareness of the baby's bodyself integration.

Touch is a personal, intimate form of communication between parent and baby. It contains the imprint of their unique relationship. It can even have a healing power, provided that there is a sympathetic or attuned communication.

In this chapter I will also emphasise the effect of the touch experience with her infant on the mother. Her body can acquire aliveness through contact with the body of the baby and this can enhance her understanding of the expressive repertoire of the baby. The multilevel contact opens up receptors within the skin and thus increases awareness of her "embodiedness" (Winnicott 1962b). It has the potential to enhance a sense of psychosomatic well-being.

The touching during infant massage can help the mother to relieve tension, enhance and integrate her bodyself image, mobilize her tense shoulders, chest and breathing, and smooth her posture (Sansone, 2004). The practice of baby massage should come naturally but sometimes it does not because of blocked emotional and muscular tension that prevents the interacting gestures from evolving. The flow of energy in the body is essential for the parent to let the massage movements evolve freely and make the massage an expression of love (Fig 1).

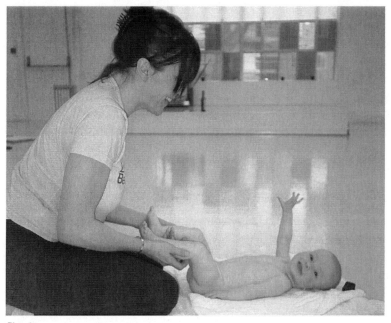

Fig. 1.

I shall examine the possible value of mindful infant massage in enhancing the relationship and communication skills of parent and infant, particularly in the case of mothers with emotional difficulties. Touching during massage connects the parent and baby in a way that is unmatched by any other type of interaction.

I am suggesting that baby massage, with the presence of a third containing, mindful person–the infant massage teacher–has the potential to facilitate "beneficial psychosomatic processes" by enriching the mother's sense of her body ego. This potential is enhanced when the sensory experiences can be explored in psychoanalytical terms. I endeavour to bring a psychoanalytic sensitiveness to such material and its meanings.

I explore here two closely connected aspects. The first concerns the infant's need for touch and movement in order to develop a sense of "indwelling" in the body (Winnicott, 1962b). The second concerns re-experienced memories that may be evoked through the mother's experience of touch with her infant. I refer to a mirroring process activated by baby massage, which has the potential to lead the mother to a regression. This re-experiencing can be explored in psychoanalytical terms.

In the clinical case presented in this book I suggest that the touch experience with her baby can enhance the mother's tolerance to closeness, by weakening her rigid defences.

During massage, mother and baby are organizing and coordinating five aspects of sensory communication–sight, touch, smell, hearing, and taste–through a sixth powerful channel of communication, which is movement. Both mother and baby are reintroduced to a familiar world of vibrations and rhythms. To do so, the mother needs to rediscover and regress to a more primitive language.

A mother may develop a "second skin" to avoid contact with her baby, who revives her non-containing primal experiences. Such a defensive skin can manifest through muscular tightening, reluctance to make eye contact, vocal tension, or lack of holding, and is experienced by the infant as a lack of physical holding and psychic containment. Baby massage can enhance the mother's awareness of her tension and of its release. Such awareness is often accompanied by the emergence of memories and feelings, as will emerge from the clinical illustration.

Where there has been a failure in being "held," this may cause the parent to be intolerant of physical contact with her or his infant. Baby massage, in addition to the containing group experience, offers a context for restoring or keeping alive a sense of being well held and ease in the body. It constitutes a safe space where memories and feelings that have been locked in the body since infancy, may be re-experienced and become accessible to elaboration. This enhances a sense of psychosomatic integration.

Whilst I avoid physical contact with clients in the counselling room, during a baby massage session I occasionally go over the mother when I notice excessive tension in her shoulders or arms, which prevents her massage movements running smoothly and firmly. I mindfully touch the tightened part of the body and sometimes I encourage her, for example, by gently supporting her back. Such "supporting touching" may trigger a process of physical "restaging" of events formed in her earliest life. This material proves very useful for work; in transference it may develop into verbal expression. As I wrote earlier these physical insights may facilitate the client's regression in a psychoanalytic setting, the process towards "feeling real', and a full sense of psychosomatic integration. Very often I find interesting associations between the mother's feelings stirred by my touching of her body and early experiences of being held.

Winnicott's 1949 paper refers to his physical facilitation of the patient's regression in the psychoanalytic setting. The patient's progress towards "feeling real" and a full sense of psychosomatic integration is accompanied by the physical restaging of events forming a part of the birthing process, as well as verbal exploration of the emerging material. I underpin his view that in certain circumstances appropriate touching can trigger important processes associated with the early holding experience. It is not my intention to suggest physical contact in the psychoanalytic setting. However, I have found it fruitful to work in the therapeutic setting with material arising from the experience of a baby massage group.

Touch and communication

Physical contact such as kissing, cuddling, holding, and stroking encourages infants to thrive. If they are deprived of this, their physical, emotional, and intellectual potential is impoverished.

Western societies have become so impersonal and desensitized to the value of loving touch that many mothers are still discouraged from expressing this from the earliest months of birth by having their babies whisked away. Depriving any mammal of the opportunity to feed or feel her offspring makes the mother likely to reject her newborn.

The newborn's baby need for physical reassurance is paramount for its healthy psychophysiological development. Touch is the most developed of the senses at birth and the primary tool of communication. It is regarded as the "mother sense" and plays a major role in the parent-child relationship. It is no coincidence that we use expressions such as "to have the feel for", or "to be in touch with" to describe human relationships in terms of our sense of touch. The way in which babies are touched and held has a remarkable effect on the development of their personality. Massage provides the best way of getting the feel of, getting to know, and becoming able to handle the baby with more confidence. It can ease the parent's as well as the infant's anxiety and increase mutual self-trust in both of them.

The benefits of a period of close physical contact are supported by research from all over the world. In his book *Touching* (1978), Ashley Montague included some anthropological observations of Balinese children and the Arapesh in New Guinea, the Netsilik Inuit of the Arctic, the Bushmen of the Kalahari, and the Ganda children of East Africa. Studies on the babies of these cultures, who are cradled, sung to, stroked, caressed, and carried by their mothers and other family members, show that their overall development appears well advanced. In her book *The Continuum Concept* (1986) Jean Liedloff reported her observational work of two and a half years living with the Yequana of South America. Liedloff has described how instinctive maternal and parental capacity (if not impaired by childhood experiences), is aroused by physical contact with the newborn baby, which also helps a parent to respond properly to the baby's emotional and physical needs.

Touch, the primary source of stimulation for the foetus, is perceived very early and enhances prenatal learning (Brazelton 1995). Touch not only stimulates growth but is also the primary source of communication with the foetus (via sound vibrations and amniotic fluid movements). Touch is also a powerful channel of communication between two individuals who love each other. Touching provides stimulation and can communicate that the world is a safe and trustworthy place. It can affect human functioning at different levels, from the simplest cell to the highest psychological levels.

A baby, who is without emotional and muscular defences, is even more responsive to the power of touch. In intensive care units, tiny and sick babies often "forget" to breathe because they are understimulated. Nurses sometimes slap their feet to stimulate them to start breathing again. This hospital routine should be substituted by more caring ways of giving stimulation.

Infant massage is a time when sensitive touch can reach powerful expression. It opens all the sensory channels, strengthens breathing, and lets any tension flow from the body out towards the periphery. When a baby is screaming with colic or another ailment, touching allows the tension concentrated in a specific area to flow throughout the body. When the baby feels pain in one part of the body, she experiences a feeling of fragmentation and all the emotional and muscle tension becomes blocked in that part. Gentle stroking can help the tension flow, reconnecting all the parts of the body in union.

A review of touch

There is considerable evidence that responsive human touch is essential both to the infant's healthy survival and to the mother's ability to nurture. In 1945, Spitz reported on the terrible consequences of inadequate handling of hospitalized infants in the US, many of whom did not survive. This fortunately led to improved conditions. Many institutions ceased to exist as laboratories for the study of touch; deprivation and further research was now carried out on primates rather than on human infants.

Harry Harlow's (1962) famous experiments with monkeys were the first to show that for infants contact comfort is even more important than food. Some monkeys were "raised" by a "wire mother" with a bottle of milk attached, while others also had a soft "terrycloth mother", to which they clung most of the time. All the monkeys were very disturbed as adults, but those who had been brought up by a "terrycloth mother" were slightly less affected than the "wire mother only" babies. Though given all the food they needed, without touch and emotional nurturing, care, and comfort, they neglected themselves and were completely inadequate as parents, often abandoning their own offspring.

Studies of the macaque monkey (Reite & Field 1985; McKenna, 1986) indicate that, when separated from their mothers, primates as old as four to six months also undergo a reduction of body temperature and can have disturbances in sleep, with decreased rapid-eye-movement sleep periods, changes in electroencephalogram activity, alterations in cellular immune responses, along with increases in cardiac arrhythmia, and adrenal (stress hormone) secretion and cortisone levels.

Evidence supports the same conclusions for us humans. When parents abuse infants by depriving them of bodily contact, babies can gradually lose weight even though they are being fed. Food intake alone is not enough to guarantee normal weight when there is no loving physical contact. Recent studies with premature babies have demonstrated that skin-to-skin ventral contact with their mothers is of tremendous benefit. "Kangaroo care" is a practice based on skin contact that allows babies to remain attached to their life-support machines but also to experience regular contact with the mother's chest. Field (1995) describes the development of premature babies who receive kangaroo care spending almost all day in close contact with their mother's body. These babies show less fluctuation in body temperature, heart rate, and respiration rate and are ready for discharge significantly earlier than control group babies. Other studies show that with kangaroo care more mothers breast-feed, and mothers feel more fulfilled about their pregnancy. The parents become deeply attached to their infants and they feel confident about caring for them.

A "preemie's" first contact with human touch brings pain–needles, probes, tubes, rough handling, and bright lights–all of a sudden after the warm protection of the womb. Many studies have proven that premature or underweight babies who are regularly and gently stroked and who regularly hear their parents" voices during their nursery stay progress rapidly in growth and development (Scafidi, Field, Schanberg, & Bauer, 1990; Thoman, Ingersoll, & Acebo, 1991; Anderson, 1991; Newman, 1980; Field et al., 1986).

Baby massage classes provided me with an interesting setting in which to observe the delicate interplay between the baby's development on all levels and the mother's ways of modulating her touch and voice. This allowed me to assess the infant's extraordinary capacity to respond to touch and body language in general, which is already formed at birth and seems to be the result of prenatal rhythmic learning. The rapid improvement in growth and development of underweight and unresponsive babies to parents' regular stroking and talking demonstrates the physical and psychological healing effects of maintaining cues of communication (Sansone, 2004, p. 26).

Studies of premature babies have demonstrated that daily massage is of tremendous benefit (Barnard & Brazelton, 1990, Field, 1995). Evidence shows that benefits are not limited to the infant; depressed mothers seem to benefit from giving massage. They perceive their infants as being easier to soothe, which enhances their confidence in handling their babies, which improves the mother-infant relationship (Field, 1995, p. 110).

Baby massage, with its multi-level communication between parent and baby–sensory, motor, and mental–can be of particular help to the growing number of babies who are born by caesarean section, born prematurely, or who have had other kinds of difficult births or developmental problems (Barnard & Brazelton, 1990; Field, 1990).

Physical contact, by inducing sensory stimulation, acts as a synchronizer that promotes the stability of the baby's breathing. Baby massage can act as a powerful regulator of the baby's respiratory system because of the richness of the mother-baby sensory exchanges that it entails. This can protect her from environmental disturbances, particularly during the first six months of life.

In *Mothers, Babies and their Body Language* (2004) I wrote that touching during massage has similar effects to the infant's sucking and licking of the mother. I have seen women with breastfeeding problems improving within a few weeks of a baby massage class. It is possible that the special closeness, skin contact, and massage movements increase the maternal prolactin levels in the same way as licking and sucking, instilling a sense of well-being in both mother and baby. This would be further proof of the psychophysiological rapport between mother and baby, which is formed prenatally, and of their communication developed through touch and other various cues. Baby massage can improve breastfeeding and enhance pleasure and motivation in mothering, fostering a constructive bonding. Prolactin is a "love" hormone; it seems to activate the close attachment between mother and baby and can be increased by loving touch.

Allowing mother and baby to stay close to each other after birth is likely to initiate and enhance sensory, hormonal, and behavioural processes as well as immune responses that attach the mother and the baby to each other, providing an experience of mutual pleasure. The physical contact promotes more attuned responsiveness.

As we have seen, Klaus, Kennell, and Klaus (1996) highlight the benefits of early contact between parents and infants immediately after birth. If the health of the mother or infant makes this early contact difficult, then support and reassurance should help parents enhance their bonding experience. They emphasise the importance of skin and eye contact in the first hour and extended hospital stay for the infant's healthy development as well as for the mother's well-being. It has been identified as leading to a progressive increase in the infant being in a quiet, alert state in response to being held by her mother. Sensitive interactions are therefore the most important triggers for attachment and bonding. Premature and prolonged deprivation of physical loving contact can thus have harmful effects on the primary relationship and on the child's development (Field, 1977; Thompson & Westreich, 1989).

Brazelton (1983) has described and filmed the large range and nuances of movements, gestures, facial expressions, and vocalizations as indicators of the baby's changing experiences with the mother. His analysis of infant movement showed that an infant's movements are transformed by human contact. The baby's movements change from jerky and uncoordinated to smooth, rhythmic, and circular in the presence of human contact.

Psychoanalytic descriptions of the consequences of a touch-deprived state complement physiological studies. Hopkins (1990) wrote of infants born to mothers who showed an aversion to physical contact: "These babies have been found to be no less cuddly than other babies are, but by a year they neither cuddle nor cling but are carried like a sack of potatoes." These infants can give a sense of themselves as a "dead weight". Hopkins described cases in which a slumped and resigned state or lack of physical vigour in the infant are a response to inadequate holding and handling, reflecting the mother's state.

It seems that the handling an infant has experienced is stored in his or her body (embodiment) and manifests through muscle tone, "aliveness", and posture. I suggest that good posture, reflecting firm (but not rigid) holding together of the body through the musculature, is related to good experiences of maternal holding and psychosomatic integration. The way in which a mother has been nurtured as a child through touch, warmth, and holding influences the way in which she touches, holds, and cares for her own baby (Hopkins, 1990). This emerges noticeably from the case illustrated in this book. Hopkins" description above reminds me of one mother coming to a baby massage class, handling and dropping her baby on the floor like a fragile doll. I learnt in the counselling room that she had not felt "held" as an infant.

Any emotional response of the baby intensely involves the whole body. His or her emotional states are imprinted in the muscles and are visible in his or her movements, gestures, and posture. For instance, the emotional state of a confident and resilient child can be directly reflected in its upright, open, and secure posture.

Hopkins" work complements Bick's (1968), suggesting that if we have not been well held, then we cannot hold ourselves well. The lack of physical vigour described by Hopkins (1990) as a response to inadequate holding and handling, reflects a slumped and resigned body/mind state, feelings of hopelessness, of passivity and of depression. The primary touching and holding in early infancy shapes adult personality and behaviour.

Winnicott's emphasis was not upon the touch and handling itself, but upon the touch and handling that responds to the needs of a particular infant at a particular time. This leads me, before starting a baby massage session, to suggest to mothers that they stop massaging when their babies show signs of discomfort or begin to cry. Winnicott described (1952, 1960a, 1960b,) the infant need in the very early stages of life for an illusion of omnipotence, for feeling that when he or she is hungry and the mother offers the breast, the infant has in fact created the breast. In the same way, when the mother comes and picks him or her up, the infant feels that he or she has determined this event. When the infant begins to experience the maternal object as separate and not entirely under his or her control, the role of the transitional object becomes of utmost importance (Winnicott, 1953). This object, which is both "me" and "not-me," is a substitute for the mother's holding and allows the infant to comfort him or herself and to tolerate the separation.

I want to turn to the benefits of the touch experience with her infant for the mother. I suggest that for a mother who is depressed as a response to a revived mind/body state associated with inadequate holding, the infant's vitality of posture and movements may provide an opportunity to develop a sense of alive self-holding, and confidence in the relationship with her baby. In other mothers, through a mirroring process, the baby's repetition of movements while being massaged may evoke memories in feeling (Klein, 1957) of the primal loving and attentive contact. In these terms, we might regard the playfulness of baby massage as primarily object related.

CHAPTER 5

Case illustration

> There is in the symptomatology an insistence on the interaction of
> psyche and soma, this being maintained as a defence against the threat
> of a loss of psyche-somatic union, or against a form of depersonalisation.
>
> (Winnicott, 1962a, p. 62)

The following case is a vivid description of how failure in having
been held herself may cause a mother's intolerance of physical
contact with her baby and how this can manifest through the
woman's use of her body. Mastitis, a breast inflammation that may
prevent a woman from breastfeeding, is seen here as a symptom of
a psychosomatic dysfunction. It represents the tip of the iceberg of
a conflict between the mother's will to breastfeed and her inability
to cope with the overwhelming feelings aroused by it.

Andrea and her baby received short-term counselling three
times a week for a period of two months.

Labour and birth

Andrea's case commenced on the day I was caught by remarkable human sounds from the labour room. The sounds were high and sharp and with their upward direction they seemed to go away from the woman's body and run through the ceiling. In my experience I have found that labour sounds are usually deep, primitive, and downward directed–towards the area that is more involved in the process, when they are emitted in tune with breathing and contractions as the baby descends through the pelvis. The outcome of labour seems to reside in a harmonious interaction of the mother's mind and body. Since it was the early stage of labour, when the contractions were not so powerful as to induce intense pain, Andrea's sounds seemed to be screams of fright. At one point, a midwife who had just left the labour room looked at me saying that this labouring woman had been behaving that way for a few hours, though she had not yet entered "physiological" labour (because there were no strong contractions).

In my experience with other cases, I have found that screaming using the neck, jaw, and chest, particularly when caused by anxiety and fear, enhances muscle tension and prevents breathing from being deep, smooth, and involving the abdomen. This type of screaming produces vibrations that travel away from the body. The tension prevents the vibrations from reaching the baby and thus facilitating the descent. I wrote (in 2004) that fear increases muscle tone throughout the body and may have paralysing effects on the labour process. The result is a distorted perception of the bodyself and consequently of the birth process. Fear can also interfere with the central nervous system and inhibit the hormone secretion necessary for the normal process of labour. As I found later on, in Andrea an idealized representation of birth, associated with high expectations, had induced fears of an unpredictable labour experience.

When the mother lets go rather than resists labour and birth, breathing unfolds smoothly as a sign of her psychosomatic connection to her baby. My feeling was thus that Andrea might not have been focusing on what was happening inside her body. A warm and softly pulsating uterus or pelvis is shaped by the mother's feelings; acting as an emotional container provides the best birth environment for the foetus (Piontelli 1992).

After two hours I was still standing by the closed door. At this stage, I cannot describe precisely the feeling that led me to pay attention to this woman's sounds. Standing there, I had a possible unconscious understanding, and a special sensitivity to her need for support. My knowledge of the "body/self image" and its relation to voice, labour, and mother-baby interactions, which was an aspect of my research and clinical work, probably enabled me to pick up some signs from analysing the labouring woman's sounds.

Voice expresses emotion by tempo, timbre, or "voice quality" (Sansone, 2004, p. 117). Voice can give us information about the degree of tension or relaxation. Tension in the motor system, in particular in the mother's throat, where her sounds are being made, also manifests in the way she holds her baby. Voice vibrations are modulated by emotions, so through them the baby connects with the mother's internal world and recognizes the quality of her emotions. The voice, its tones, and energy level communicate emotion and have a direct effect on the baby. Movements, gestures, eye contact, and voice tone are all conditioned by emotions. For instance, a depressive state characterized by low muscular tone manifests itself through slow movements, a flat, low-pitched, monotonous voice, and reduced eye contact.

Excessive anxiety may result from an element of disconnection between mind and body. Since anxiety expresses itself through the tone and speed of voice, voice is thus an expression of the bodyself image. A mother's attitude to her body and self during pregnancy, labour, and birth will not only contribute to shaping the quality of her holding, and massaging, but also of how she talks to her baby and of every moment of contact.

Meanwhile another midwife was leaving the labour room. She said that the labour was becoming complicated and that the woman had to have an epidural. The contractions had increasingly slowed down and become sporadic. Several hours later, there was no change in the dilation of the cervical opening. I have noted that an increasing number of women request an epidural either because they find the pain unbearable or because the fear of not being able to manage the unpredictable labour is too overwhelming.

Despite the anaesthetic effect, the woman kept emitting acute screams from time to time. Then silence descended, probably between two contractions, sometimes followed by a few words, and the sound of her voice began to vibrate through the wall again.

I recognised the obstetrician's voice, who must have been advising her of some more suitable position to facilitate the baby's descent through the pelvis. Normally there is only a midwife in the labour room. The obstetrician intervenes either in the case of an emergency or when the couple have chosen the consultant package (which is more expensive and implies more frequent check-ups) instead of the midwife package. I could also hear her partner's voice and recognise the midwife manager's voice. It is quite unusual at the Birth Unit (where privacy is one of the guiding principles), for a labouring woman to be surrounded by such numerous staff. It seemed she expected and needed a big audience to draw attention to herself.

After a lunch break, I returned to the Birth Unit to see another patient who had delivered the day before and with whom I had followed-up since early pregnancy. When I left this woman's room, I was asking a midwife about the labouring woman, when I saw another midwife carry a ventous into the labour room. It had become necessary to get the baby out. (This medical intervention is carried out when the baby's head is engaged in the pelvic canal but cannot progress.)

In labour, breathing, labour contractions, and gravity need to work in synchronization. Fear and anxiety are associated with altered breathing. To let her body be guided by the process of labour, a woman needs to feel and balance gravity effectively. In order to respond to that need, it is worth finding support in her feet and a steady grounding. The psychosomatic integration and conscious perception of the bodyself can enable a woman to be led by gravity and by her breathing, as if by a sea current. Resistance to the flow of gravity however, may prevent the uterine muscles from stretching, relaxing, and contracting alternately, and the pelvis from dilating in rhythm with the breathing and the baby's movements (Sansone, 2004, p. 109).

The capacity to find effective support in our bodyself is connected with self-trust and takes shape during our primary experiences. The special attachment that develops between mother and baby is the baby's first experience of being entirely loved and of trusting another human being. This unique relationship builds the foundation of the child's capacity to trust his or her body-mind and the way he or she will relate to other people.

When I acknowledge the importance of the birth environment and appropriate emotional support for the labouring woman to feel secure, I believe that self-trust or self-holding is an essential key and is built on our primary relationship through a fulfilling experience of being held, and trusting our parents.

The baby was immediately whisked out just outside the labour room and placed into a cot to be helped in its breathing through an oxygen machine. This triggered a call to a neonatologist to check the baby. I walked towards the cot to see the newborn baby and asked the obstetrician about the woman's condition. As the labour door was ajar, I could recognise the woman from her voice: it was Andrea.

A few hours later, a midwife walked towards me handing the baby out to let me see her. I held the baby, who did not seem to show particular signs of distress due to the difficult birth. She appeared to rest comfortably wrapped in the towel.

Prenatal

Having been present on the ward during the labour, I recall the portrait of Andrea that my observations had drawn during the prenatal classes. Those came to my mind clearly and strikingly. (A description of it is relevant to this woman's use of her body and its relation to her mental state.) The first time I saw Andrea in a prenatal class when she was nearly four months pregnant, she showed remarkable self-confidence and pride in her posture and movements, and an ecstatic enjoyment about her pregnancy.

She maintained this attitude throughout pregnancy. In her late pregnancy, no sign of the tiredness or discomfort that most women commonly show came from either her posture or facial expressions. Instead, she proudly assumed some flexible ballerina poses, which she evidently liked to display in front of the group (later on I learnt that she had studied ballet). She used to come to the class and chat with other women, and then she sat on the cushion, opened her pelvis wide and stretched her legs on the floor leaning her chest forwards. Observing her posture and body language gave me the impression that she was wearing her body like a beautiful dress to exhibit. Once, while talking to the group, she commented that her pregnancy had been as wonderful and perfect as she had always expected.

Andrea's attention directed mostly outwards made me think of difficulties in her psychosomatic integration. Donald Winnicott (1958a) beautifully described the mother's "reverie" as a state in which she appears absent from the world around her. Her reverie emerges from thinking intensely about her baby during pregnancy, which helps her to identify with her baby's needs after birth.

I want to draw attention to Andrea's way of speaking rapidly while avoiding eye contact. During the prenatal class run by a midwife/family therapist she was asked to talk about her feelings, and her communication with her baby (the topic of the session), but she jumped from that subject to talking about her husband or indeed anything else. Andrea tended to describe anything concerning pregnancy and birth as perfect and in an idyllic way, without ever mentioning her emotional or actual experiences. In only one instance did she address the question of communication with her baby, and said, "It's not necessary to speak up to your baby..." Then she instantly changed the subject, leaving me to wonder about what other kinds of communication she was alluding to.

I saw in Andrea's idealization of pregnancy a warning sign of a lack of contact with the real baby. I have written in detail elsewhere (Sansone, 2004) that the mother's ability to attune to her own bodily rhythms allows her to nurture a mental representation of the baby that is closer to the real individual baby.

Andrea's apparent confidence turned out to be the thick shell of an "idyllic" pregnancy, which she needed to develop to compensate for a difficult early life. I learnt later on during our meetings how well such a defence mechanism could be used to deny unbearable emotions related to early experiences (Freud, 1905). At that stage, when I was merely observing her during the prenatal classes, I did not have a clear understanding that her manifested confidence was a sign of defence and disconnection with her emotional life. However, I did sometimes notice signs of overcontrol and defence mechanisms.

Post-natal

The day after Andrea's delivery I was going to visit her in her room, when I saw a dressed-up middle-aged woman approaching the same room. She said a cool "Hello', without even turning her face to me or to the midwives who were standing by the reception, and walked straight into the room. After about twenty minutes this woman left the room and I heard from a midwife that she was Andrea's mother.

Reassured that there were no other visitors in the room, I knocked on the door, and after Andrea's "Come in', I entered. She showed a hint of surprise in her tone of voice and facial expression, but appeared to be delighted to see me. She welcomed me in a friendly way, as if she had already established a certain relationship with me during the prenatal sessions, though I had always related to the group she attended as "just" an observer. I ascribe her behaviour to my empathic perception of her state. Her baby Rosy was lying awake in the perspex cot. I walked towards the baby to look at her. I had not yet taken a seat when Andrea went straight through her birth story. "I had some problems due to the baby's position, but everything went well in the end. In the labour room there were the people I expected to be, Raphael (the consultant obstetrician), Clare (the midwife manager), Helen (the midwife on duty) whose strong and alive personality I like very much", said Andrea.

Andrea's friendly feelings towards me make me think of the transference that she began to form earlier on during the antenatal classes. I was struck by Andrea's way of viewing her birth experience with extreme optimism and control. Her language had a "faraway" quality and she did not turn her face to her baby while talking. Then she indulged herself talking about the obstetrician. "Raphael has a strong personality, like me. Sometimes he is hard, but he can also be soft and nice", she said. Then she mentioned their frequent arguments during her prenatal check-ups, in particular the one concerning "nutrition". As a consequence, she did not want to see him for some time. "But I like him. I needed him to be present during my labour but with the one condition that he would be really interested, not because he was on duty," Andrea pointed out.

Andrea's friendly and at the same time conflicting feelings towards the obstetrician guided me to seeing him as a transference object for her, an important source for inference about her state of mind, primal relationship, use of her body, and her appearance.

While talking, Andrea did not make any eye contact. I had noticed this during the prenatal classes, when she always looked away from the group leader. Her eyes, now rolling, then up and down, wide open, moved round quickly, while she went on saying that things in her life had always gone right. She told me that she usually found the right people in the right place, and that on that day, for example, the midwife who helped her deliver was the one she liked most. Then she went back to talking about the obstetrician, pointing to the bunch of flowers he had sent as a birth gift. Again, the directions and movements of her eyes did not show any signs of reflective moments, which women usually show while telling their birth story.

I noticed that Andrea had not mentioned her feelings and body experiences during labour at all, such as breathing or contractions, pain, worry, or any aspect of her baby's behaviour while coming into the world. As I wrote earlier on, her language had a "faraway" quality and felt quite distancing. There was evidently a denial of reality expressing itself through a tendency to over control and idealize it. Idealization can here be seen as a mental process to protect Andrea and lead her away from her true body ego.

At one point, Andrea asked me to pick up her baby and almost immediately she said, "Rosy likes you, she remembers you very well', alluding to when I had held her a few hours after birth. Then she got out of bed, sat on the rocking chair next to me and prepared for breastfeeding. I held Rosy out to her, and then she lifted her top and adjusted the baby to her breast.

She displayed an imposing, rigid, upright posture, lacking the slightest rounding of the chest that would have been a sign of containment of the feeding baby. The arm holding the baby looked contracted and fairly geometrical. Her fingers, spread out to hold the tiny head, revealed some tension. This, together with her shoulders, formed the picture of a ballerina pose. I did not see any sign of slight discomfort in her facial expressions or immobile shoulders, as I have seen in most women the very first days they breastfeed, due either to early milk expulsion or unknown breastfeeding positions. Nor did I see any change in her facial expression. From time to time she said repeatedly, "Sweetie! Sweetie! Sweetie!" without looking at the baby at all.

I highlight the importance of the mother's varying facial expressions and tones of voice and eye contact, to facilitate the communication with the baby and promote her overall development. All this is a form of "dancing" with the baby, which means meeting her needs, getting in tune with her cues and pace, in short, being "receptive". The mother's vocal tones and facial expressions resonate and amplify the intensity and duration of the affective states in both members of the dyad. The mother's eye contact is a source of security, pleasure, and vitality.

Murray and Trevarthen (1985) pioneered experiments with "still-face" and "double-video". First, mother and baby communicated happy moments with vivid expressions and the baby produced many different expressions in response to the mother and looked very happy. This was then recorded in a one-minute video. The recording is a perfect copy, but it produces only a depressive state in the baby, who looks confused and disturbed. The baby seeks live conversation with coordinated and expressive bodily responses that require equally rich and expressive responses from the mother.

I reflected on Andrea's tendency to speak fast and endlessly, even while breastfeeding. At one point during the session (as I felt that this manner was tending to draw my attention away from the baby), I diverted my eyes and focused upon the baby and noticed that her eyes were closed and she seemed to be dozing at the breast, just giving the occasional suck. As the session approached the end, I decided to leave the pair alone, hoping they could share this intimate moment. I departed from the visit slightly anxious and tired.

Investigations by both Andrea and myself were opened up by our transference and countertransference. I began to understand Andrea's defences, such as her tendency to hand her baby to me, or to speak fast without making eye contact, as information contributing further to the understanding of her mind/body state. I became a recipient of some of the projections that go backwards and forwards between mother and baby. Over time, as I saw the intimate links between psychoanalytic interpretation and bodily aspects (such as breastfeeding posture, volume of milk, lack of eye contact, type of intonation, and voice rhythms), I came to understand mastitis as quintessentially psychosomatic, with the ability to communicate something of value.

A few days after birth

Andrea left the Birth Unit a few days later. I was talking to a midwife when I heard a woman cry desperately and loudly from down the corridor. The midwife noticed my expression of wonder at seeing Andrea back and said, "It must be post-natal depression," sounding resigned in her tone, meaning "the so-common post-natal depression".

Later on I heard from another midwife that Andrea had developed mastitis and needed to spend a few days at the hospital.

The day after Andrea's return to the hospital, I was going to visit her, when I saw her walk towards me holding her baby out. She did not look at the baby while doing so or before turning towards the room in a "bye bye" gesture. I focused on Andrea's way of giving me Rosy straightaway without asking. She just explained that she needed a shower and while walking away she said, "I would like you to be my childminder." After half an hour she left the room and walked back and forth down the corridor to reception a few times. While doing so, she held her sore breasts with both hands looking as if she was carrying a tray with crystal glasses in the middle of the air.

The next day, while approaching Andrea's room, I saw a midwife who had just visited her show signs of discomfort and powerlessness. She glanced at me and claimed, "It is a difficult case".

Mastitis, which was hindering Andrea breastfeeding, had become a major medical problem for the midwives and the obstetrician. During my work with Andrea and Rosy I sometimes noted a sense of powerlessness on the part of the midwives. I quietly commented that on some occasions, they gave me the impression that, armed with questions about the frequency of infant feeds and about the intake of medicines, they may have indeed been felt by the new mother to be trying, for instance, to teach her "how to hold her baby", or "to be careful with positioning" while breastfeeding, or to feed her baby often. I am reminded of Winnicott's strong views about the difficulties of intervening in the parent-infant relationship. He believed that you cannot teach a mother how to hold her baby, but you can talk to her instead of the importance of providing a holding environment to facilitate her capacity to care for the infant (Winnicott, 1988, 1991).

On another visit, as I opened the door Andrea appeared to be delighted to see me from her bright "Hello!" Rosy was lying on the bed next to the mother's left side. A midwife asked her in which arm she would like to get the needle. Andrea reluctantly offered her left arm while saying, "I do not need this drug." I noticed the link between her left arm tied to the tube delivering medication and how it prevented her from holding her baby.

As I approached the baby to say "Hello", Andrea brightened up. She invited me to pick up Rosy. I accepted, hoping to offer a mirroring image for her. As I prepared my arms to hold the baby I felt this time that I had to bear the full impact of Rosy's unmet psychological needs, her distress, and her disturbance. These were only too evident in her lack of liveliness, her slumped posture, and her pallid and tired appearance. Her eyes were open but vacant and unfocused. Rosy seemed to have picked up on feelings of weariness and inadequacy. Like her mother, she seemed emotionally depleted and lacking in physical energy. This gave me a more detailed picture of a slumped and resigned body/mind state, which Hopkins (1990) describes as a lack of physical vigour due to inadequate holding and handling.

Numerous studies illustrate the sensitivity of young infants to the quality of their interpersonal engagement. The infant internalizes the mother's mental state and the reciprocal effects on the relationship, which impinges on his or her development (Murray & Stein, 1991; Murray, 1997a; Murray, 1997b).

During the same session, Andrea told me that she had always refused to take drugs and made a gesture of nearly taking the tube off. She expressed her rejection with a certain degree of anger. She stated that she certainly did not want to give any "drugs" to Rosy (she meant formula milk). Yet mastitis was preventing her from breastfeeding. Then she said, "I wanted an active birth as I believe in nature. I have always thought that the best gift I could give my baby would be breast milk."

Throughout her pregnancy Andrea had planned to breastfeed and now she was disappointed and discouraged by her inability to do so. I tried to reassure her, saying that she had lots of gifts to offer her baby such as holding, touching, and cuddling, which were indeed more important and nourishing than the milk itself. I explained that several studies have shown that continued close contact is fundamental for the child's sense of security and her healthy development. I said "They have found, and so have I, in my experience, that keeping the baby close to the mother's body in the first months of life has just as positive effect as does breastfeeding".

For the first time Andrea was silent. Her face turned pale and her voice slowed and was trembling. She was close to crying but tried to hold it in. I saw in this abrupt change, dramatically visible through her body language, a "turning point', a central aspect of the transference phenomena at work. I felt something moving inside me as well. It was as if we were embarking onto a deeper understanding and connection, based on empathic perception and similar to that pursued in meditative practice. I want to explain the importance of the therapist's capacity to let go or be changed to allow for transformation in the client. This "constructive" process in the therapist is usually kept at bay in Western psychology and psychotherapy. I realized later that that "change" could powerfully illuminate the way in which the mother's experience of the infant was organized. (The collection of information about Andrea's earliest relationships and the progress of transference will make sense of this turning point).

Over time I came to see mastitis not as Andrea's central problem but merely as a psychosomatic symptom, a mind/body strategy to avoid close physical contact with her baby and the unbearable anxieties stirred by it. This was consistent with her tendency to put me in charge of holding Rosy, always giving an excuse, for instance, that she needed a shower. In her determination to breastfeed there seemed to be anger, a struggle, and a sense of failure at not being able to perform it. I am constantly illuminated by Winnicott's thoughts that the mother's milk does not flow like an excretion. It is a response to a variety of elements: the sight, smell, feeling, and thinking of the baby. I was reminded of the "thinking breast" described by Bion (1962b). The periodic feeding develops as a communication between mother and baby based on a rhythmical exchange of cues, a song without words, or a dance, in which the infant needs to be fed and comforted are both met.

Bion (1962a) highlighted the baby's need for interaction with the mother to experience self. The mother's reverie, giving the baby permission to experience through interactions with her, helps the baby acknowledge and accept all the parts of his or herself as a whole. This is crucial for the formation of a realistic sense of bodyself (Sansone, 2004).

Another theme derives from Andrea's tendency to have repeated showers (regardless of whether she really needed one). On one visit, she described the sensation of the running water on her bare skin as a caress, and her pleasure in swimming. I was reminded of Winnicott's work on handling (1962a). One apparent meaning of showers or swimming for Andrea was the maintenance of a sensual sense of self, which depends upon physical rather then upon verbal self-expression. This is consistent with Andrea's incapacity to verbalize her emotions in terms of psychosomatic experience. The contact with water may have been related to sensuality, to reclaiming early experiences of benign maternal care, and to reaching towards a sense of physical well-being, which she lacked. It can be seen as intrinsic both to self-care and to a reassessment of the maternal care that she did not receive.

Winnicott (1949) explained that the future mother's capacity to integrate the regressive feelings brought about by pregnancy with outer reality is associated with a psyche-soma that loves and works in harmony with itself.

It seems clear that in Andrea the inner ideal child nurtured during pregnancy was still alive, preventing her from accepting and connecting with the real baby. Thailand offers an interesting example of the way the adjustment to birth and post-natal period is handled. For centuries Thai women, upon becoming pregnant, have purchased a clay statue of a mother and infant. At the time of birth the statue is thrown into the river; thus the image of the mother and infant is literally destroyed, to be replaced by reality (Klaus, Kennell, & Klaus, 1996). Klaus, Kennell and Klaus highlight the benefits of early contact between parents and infants immediately after birth and that if the health of the mother or infant makes this early contact difficult, then support and reassurance should help parents enhance their bonding experience.

The phantasmatic child that I identified in Andrea is the unconscious construction that parents may make of the child, derived primarily from the parent's unresolved conflicts with her/his own parents. Instead the imaginary child is the conscious construction that parents make out of characteristics that they perceive or wish for the child. Neither the phantasmatic child or the imaginary child correspond to the actual child. Because the existence of the phantasmatic child may jeopardize bonding and thus the actual baby's development, it is important to identify this process, as it may well become the cause of difficulties. When the parents are helped to recognize their unconscious constructions and to make them conscious, they become less likely to interfere with the real child's healthy development.

During the same visit, after the pause of silence, Andrea nodded and said, "I know, but Steven (her husband) believes in the benefits of breast milk and is very concerned now." I could see the burden of her sense of guilt.

During one of our meetings in which Steven was present, I received the impression that Andrea's description of him "being concerned" was not objective. He seemed to be reasonably receptive to the whole issue of providing other nurturing "gifts" to the baby as more important than the milk itself.

Thinking of Andrea's mastitis and her tendency to avoid physical contact with her baby, it occurred to me to wonder whether she had suffered from a lack of emotional containment in her childhood.

At one point in the same session, I remarked to Andrea that her breastfeeding problems might be a symptom of a difficulty between her and her baby. I explained that when a parent is distressed it often seems that echoes of painful childhood experiences have been stirred up by the birth of the baby. I told her that her mastitis could be seen as just the tip of the iceberg of this turmoil of pregnancy and the neonatal period. I also suggested that the breast symptom could be seen as a positive force, helping her understand the connection between the problems in the present and her early life. I told her that understanding the meaning of the use of her body would allow her to establish an healthy interaction of mind and body, leading to her adjustment to the baby's needs. "I will try to support you and the baby and help you smooth the very important steps in adjusting to Rosy. My aim is also to help you see yourself as healthy and ready to mother your baby", I said.

The "key moment" guided me to the point where it became natural to ask her about her parents. She was also guided to the same point, where she naturally felt able to reveal her earliest experiences with her parents. I asked for information on what she felt was relevant about her childhood and her relationships with her parents. I did not ask specific questions, which could have been perceived as intrusive. My communication seemed to penetrate her aura of vagueness and to touch her. It brought to mind memories and feelings, long forgotten. Bit by bit, Andrea began to recall her history of a lack of touch and emotional deprivation in childhood.

I had not even finished formulating my questions when Andrea started telling me about her mother (after shaking her head), drawn back to an early set of memories. "What I remember of her is going out with a friend and walking around to look at the shops. She never stayed at home and never had time to hug or cuddle me", Andrea said with a hint of anger. For the first time I heard how unhappy she felt. In her words "She never stayed at home", I saw a sense of physical abandonment, of feeling desperately lonely and unhappy and of longing to be held and comforted. Recalling these experiences prompted a welling-up of feelings of sadness, vulnerability, and, most of all, anger, as it transpires from the following passage.

Then she told me that her sister was the sort of person who did not mind taking drugs, and having sex without any precautions and yet, to her mother she has always been the perfect daughter. From this description a feeling of enormous rage towards her sister emerged. Andrea also seemed envious of her, as from her perspective, her mother had so much more time and love for her sister then she did for her.

At this point I recalled a midwife telling me that when Andrea's mother came to the hospital to see Rosy after birth she did not touch the baby but just said repeatedly, "Sweetie! Sweetie, Sweetie!" Strikingly, the midwife's mimic sounded precisely like Andrea's words "Sweetie! Sweetie!" while breastfeeding during my earliest visits.

McDougall (1989) argued that people who develop psychosomatic symptoms, as a result of their incapacity to elaborate verbally their emotional suffering, unconsciously evoke in others (by their ways of talking and acting), the feelings that they themselves have repudiated. In fact they frequently talk and act in the way their parents did when they were little. Because emotions are psychosomatic, their incapacity to be in touch with a child's emotional needs may lead the child to develop the symptom as a defence against emotional suffering.

My uncertainties, which had been generated initially by Andrea's preoccupations, defences, and symptoms, were gradually being resolved by a recognition that the material corresponded to an already familiar pattern. This process unfolded simultaneously, with Andrea's recognition of this important connection between her earliest relationships and the present and, as a consequence, with the weakening of her ego defences.

Bearing in mind her ballerina pose while breastfeeding, I asked Andrea about her experience as a dancer. She told me that she began studying ballet when she was very young but had to give it up due to knee problems. When she recovered she took up contemporary dance, which she enjoyed very much. "But my mother wanted me to be a successful ballerina', she pointed out, while touching her swollen sore red breast and making an expression of pain.

The simultaneity of her gesture and what she was saying left me wondering about the association between her mastitis and her knee problems, and therefore about Andrea's unconscious use of her body. The gesture of touching her breast was now accompanied by her words, "Raphael (the obstetrician) should see my breasts now!" The simultaneity of her gestures and words, while she was talking about her mother, provided further inference about Andrea's transference with the obstetrician. Then she stared at and touched the vein in her left arm while she complained about it being badly inflamed due to the needle and the injected medicine. While doing so, a midwife who had just come in to check her condition said, "There is nothing but just a red tiny mark. You always exaggerate, Andrea."

I think of Andrea's inner scar (lack of early holding and touching) that made her perceive the needle's mark as a big injury. I also reflect upon her use of her body to avoid contact with her true feelings and needs by developing a symptom. Did perhaps the knee problems express her rebellion at her mother's control over her body and her inability to meet her needs? A child's self-model is profoundly influenced by how the mother perceives him or her (Hopkins, 1990). Whatever she fails to recognise, he or she is likely to fail to recognise in him or herself. In this way major parts of a personality can be split off and unintegrated.

I reflect upon Andrea's feeling of failure and guilt about not being able to please her mother. Some painful memories about her father now came to light. "He worked in the Armed Forces and was an alcoholic. He liked going out with different women. He used to say that I was not a good daughter. When he died, in 1989, I didn't want to go to his funeral. But when I got married I felt proud of him for the first time when signing his name', she said.

It occurred to me to wonder whether, by getting married, my client could reframe her impaired male model, forgive her father, and lighten her sense of guilt. But ghosts of the past had came back, when, for instance, she felt that her husband was angry with her for not being able to breastfeed. Her feeling of failure and guilt were acting in the present and affecting her mind/body functioning.

Naturally, there are many psychoanalytic considerations to take into account when exploring such material and I can only refer to the ones related to bodily functioning and psychosomatic disturbance. It is relevant to see how transgenerational models may act in the present through a psychosomatic symptom such as mastitis. Andrea's unconscious working model about her baby Rosy was derived from what she had picked up as a very young infant. This misperception and identification with her child-self had been recreated in her pregnancy and birth of her baby.

The belief that parenting patterns are passed on may be well founded. Many studies have revealed that the way in which we are cared for and nurtured as infants and children affects how we parent, as well as how we interact with other people in general (Klaus, Kennell, & Klaus, 1996).

The way in which a mother was nurtured as a child through touch, warmth, and holding influences the way in which she touches, holds, and cares for her own baby (Hopkins, 1990). This emerges noticeably from Andrea's case.

The perinatal period, pregnancy, and postpartum period can make early experiences resurface unexpectedly, without the parent being able to recognize their source or their effect on how they monitor their bodyself. The success of breastfeeding or bottle-feeding is partly dependent on the way in which a woman copes with the emotional surge aroused during her transition to motherhood.

Bowlby (1979) and Winnicott have documented how a parent's own mothering becomes an inner model for their own future care taking. Ghosts of past experiences in early life can deeply affect parental feelings and behaviours (Fraiberg, 1980). Thus long before a woman herself becomes a mother, she has learned from the way she was mothered and through observation, play, and practice a repertoire of mothering behaviours. These behaviours are taken in by the child through a complex mental process and become unquestioned imperatives throughout life. I want to shine a light on the "embodiedness" of this mental process. Unless adults consciously re-examine these internalized attitudes, they will unconsciously repeat them when they become parents through the use of their bodies.

Learning occurs together with feelings and dramatically involves the body and the muscle memory. This is especially visible in the young baby, whose learning involves the whole body in a dramatic way. What we learn in our earliest life is recorded in our feelings and muscle memory and it manifests in our posture, gestures, and the way we deal with relationships (Sansone, 2004). For example, a baby records the mother's voice not just by hearing it but also, and more importantly, by sensing the vibrations and rhythm of the sounds in her skin and muscles. She records its emotional quality. In the same way, the baby records the emotional quality of the mother's gestures. Together with her touch, eye contact, facial expression, and smell, the mother's voice modulates the baby's muscular and emotional activities, as well as other physiological activities, such as respiratory, cardiac, and digestive functions, and by doing so she shapes the baby's posture, gestures, and behaviours.

Andrea was evidently projecting onto her baby her inner child, and the way she had been mothered, whilst at the same time trying hard to voice her rebellion towards her mother. She had retreated from emotional involvement with herself and her baby by avoiding physical contact, perhaps because she was afraid that her interactions would have reminded her of the frustrating breast she had encountered as a young child and of the shame of needing the breast. This may also explain her tendency to avoid eye contact. Perhaps she had withdrawn from an emotional life due to the fear of being dominated by, and dependent on, the breast that had frustrated her.

I recall thinking over time of Andrea's peculiar pose while breastfeeding during our first meetings. Her arms and shoulders appeared immobile and stiff and her posture resembled that of a ballerina pose. They did not show any soft curving that would have been a sign of containment of the baby. In time, I came to associate this posture with a "second skin" manifesting itself through muscular tightening. It may have contributed to the development of mastitis.

In *Mothers, Babies and their Body Language* (2004) I wrote that the release of milk can be altered by the mother's emotions and how she relates to her bodyself image, whether she is comfortable with her physical and emotional changes or is struggling. Emotions display themselves through muscular tone and gestures and can affect milk release not only at a cerebral level (in the hypothalamus) but also at a peripheral level, by interfering with the muscular canal inside the breast. This muscle needs to be working in rhythm with the baby's sucking, and also in harmony with the mother's shoulders and chest muscles, her breathing, and her whole posture. I describe this process as a dance of muscles. In other words, the communication, whether at bodily or verbal level, is characterized by rhythmic exchanges.

All the intricate interactions involving the baby's sucking, which affect the mother's hormones, activate a milk response, enhance maternal feelings, free her body language, deepen receptiveness, perpetuate, and shape an age-old human cycle.

Subsequent to the visit during which Andrea gave me a portrait of her family, I asked her if she would like to describe her feelings while she was breastfeeding. Again, she gave me details of her ideal word but without a hint of her emotional experience. "When I went back home after delivery (three days after), before getting mastitis I used to breastfeed on a "Victorian bed", imagine, with lots of cushions and in a ballerina pose. And now…lots of problems', Andrea commented. I am struck by the link between my perception of her breastfeeding posture and her description.

Another theme derives from Andrea's idealistic description of breastfeeding. I am reminded of McDougall's work with patients incapable of verbally elaborating affective experiences (1989). McDougall reconstructed with these patients the existence of a paradoxical mother-child relationship in which the mother was felt to be out of touch with her child's emotional needs. She wrote that because emotions are psychosomatic, the failure to be in touch with the child's emotional needs may lead the child to recourse to the primitive mechanisms of splitting and projective identification to protect herself from being overwhelmed by mental suffering. Psychosomatic symptoms could therefore be an expression of the incapacity to elaborate and represent verbally emotional suffering.

At one point, I remarked to Andrea that, in describing her breastfeeding experience, she seemed to be drawing my attention to some kind of loss or lack in relation to her feelings and bodily experience. Like in the "key moment" described earlier on, this communication seemed to penetrate her aura of vagueness and to touch her. It brought to mind memories and feelings of having her real needs unmet. Bit by bit, Andrea began to recall her history of touch deprivation in later childhood: "She only cared for dressing me up, like a doll. These were the only moments when her hands touched me. I had to do what she wanted. She never forgave me for not being a successful ballerina."

Some very painful memories that had not been worked through for years and years came to light. She recalled a sense of physical abandonment, of feeling desperately lonely and unhappy, and of a longing to be held and comforted: "When my father returned from work I wished to be cuddled, but he was always drunk, as after work he used to go to a pub. He would say "You have been naughty. You are not a good daughter", Andrea recalled. Her tone of voice became very intense and slow, the colour of her face changed and she was close to crying. For the first time, I heard how unhappy she had felt. For the first time her words did not sound "far away" from her bodily feelings. The long pause of silence and the downward direction of her eyes gave me the feeling that a reliving of earlier experiences was occurring. These were all signs of the healing process: the reacting, instead of repression, of the bodily feelings–a reconciliation of psyche and soma. This aspect will be highlighted in Chapter Six (An East/West Approach to Working with Parents and Infants and the Healing Relationship.)

On the same visit I realized that the mother's preoccupation with her concerns had drawn my attention away from Rosy. I looked at the baby then and noticed that she appeared tiny, manifested poor motor behaviour, and sluggish, flat emotional behaviour. Rosy was staring at the ceiling, giving me a sense of developing a "second skin," responding to the baby's need for self-holding. I could see the link between the maternal mind/body state and the neonate's very early mind/body state and behaviour. They seemed to share the same early lack of physical/emotional holding.

In Murray's study on post-natal depression (1997b), the importance of maternal preoccupation on infant and child development was examined. The infant appears to internalize the mother's trauma, representations, and the reciprocal effects on the actual relationship, which impinges upon his or her development.

As Andrea began working through memories and feelings of early experiences, I thought that an important step would be to encourage her to hold her baby, and to make skin and eye contact. This would help the mother face her emotions and feelings of strangeness towards Rosy, rather than fleeing them by entrusting Rosy to someone else. I believed that the mutual interactions, through skin-to-skin contact, eye contact, cuddling, massaging, and talking, would give the mother a sense of the infant's actual experience and allow her to reflect back and mirror what she felt her infant's experience to be. I proposed the Kangaroo technique and baby massage after having explained their benefits. My goal was to facilitate the establishment of the biological regulatory system of the mother-infant dyad, so that synchronization could facilitate attuned communication and interaction. In the same way, working with parents and infants is a process of sensing and communicating emotional states alongside the exploration of meanings.

Touched by Rosy's state of abandonment, I walked towards the bed where she was lying, stroked her hands while smiling at her, and turned to Andrea, who was sitting on the armchair. I said "Don't waste your time struggling with yourself for not being able to give her your milk. She needs your presence, your love, holding, and touching far more than your milk. As long as you struggle, your baby and yourself miss something irreplaceable and vital for her development." Rosy smiled back to me while stretching out her hands to me. Andrea looked at her smiling, perhaps for the first time so intensely, and turning to me, she said in a new tone of voice, "She wants to come in your arms", while I saw in her face an underlying desire to pick her up. Then I picked up Rosy and put her in her mother's arms. Rosy slowly turned her head to gaze at her mother's face and listen to her voice, and then emitted some vocalizations.

I emphasise the impact of the mother's voice on her baby. Voice is not just heard but sensed by the baby. Listening to her mother's voice is an experience of contact, which has the same effect as touching and can have the power of modulating the mother-infant relationship, just like an orchestral conductor. Voice consists of sounds or vibrations producing muscle tone vibrations in the speaker *and* in the listener. Vibrations are modulated by emotions, so through them the baby connects with the mother's internal world and recognises the quality of her emotions (Sansone, 2004, p. 118). The voice, its tones and energy level, communicate emotion and have a direct effect on the baby. Movements, gestures, eye contact, and the voice are all conditioned by emotions. For instance, a depressive state characterized by low muscular tone, manifests itself through slow movements, a flat, low-pitched, and monotonous voice, and reduced eye contact. The baby senses the mother's emotions through her vocal and muscular vibrations, and through her body language in general.

It really seemed that Andrea was meeting her baby for the first time, whilst Rosy seemed to recognise her face and voice. Deprived of attentive face-to-face interactions with her mother, she had hitherto mainly heard her voice and looked at her from some distance. I felt that much silent communication was occurring between mother and baby and between us. Thinking that it was a delicate moment for them, I quietly departed saying "Bye, bye." This "turning point" gave me a vivid experience of the powerful identifications and triangular mirroring process.

After the "turning point', I saw increasing evidence of her internalization of my interest in her baby and in her. She became able to allow herself to "enjoy" the holding of the baby. This enjoyment may be linked to the mother's acceptance of her inability to breastfeed, her self-holding, and the enjoyment of her physicality. Winnicott comments that what is important for the baby is not the softness of the clothes and having the bath water at just the right temperature, but the mother's pleasure that goes with the clothing and bathing of her.

After nine visits, this mother-baby "meeting" gave me the first opportunity to see Rosy in an alert state. Klaus, Kennell and Klaus (1996) placed an emphasis on the importance of skin and eye contact in the first hour and extended hospital stay for the infant's healthy development as well as for the mother's well-being. It has been identified as leading to a progressive increase in the infant's being in a quiet, alert state in response to being held by her mother. Holding, cuddling, soothing, sensing, and comforting one's baby are special experiences, and whether the baby is breast or bottle fed, this communication is present if the baby is held close in the parent's arms.

There is an adaptive fit between parent-baby contact and their bodily cues (McKenna, 1986; Trevarthen, 2001b). Sensitive interactions are therefore the most important triggers for attachment and bonding. On the same line of thought, when an adult is attentive and responsive, the infant will (if not tired or hungry), show a wide and rich repertoire of gestures, facial expressions, and vocalizations that are readily apprehended by parents as communications (Trevarthen, 1979).

It is relevant to this book that physical/emotional holding is vital for the healthy psychosomatic development of infants, in which the use of their bodies and posture is rooted. This is evident in Andrea's use of her body and in her psychosomatic symptom, as well as in Rosy's poor motor behaviour and staring at the ceiling.

Parent's bodies, especially the mother's, act as a regulator of the baby's breathing, body temperature, and heart rate, particularly with premature and underweight babies. There is much research and observation to show the different ways in which parents and infants affect each other physiologically, socially, and psychologically (Schore, 1994; Feldman, Greenbaum, & Yirmiya, 1999; Trevarthen, 1999).

Andrea's awareness that mastitis was not her key problem increased over time. After that first "sensitive" contact, I saw Andrea interact with her little girl increasingly during three more visits. She made regular eye contact with Rosy and appeared to enjoy their interactions and union. Their interactions began to have some joyful teasing moments and a few smiles were seen. Somehow Andrea and Rosy were achieving and maintaining more mutual gazes. During one of the last meetings she told me that she found massaging her baby quite "playful".

Mutual gazes, eye contact, and smiling are powerful elements that help establish bonding between parent and infant. Another element is enjoyment; what ties a baby into social interaction is making it pleasurable.

I do believe that the infant massage group experience and the presence of a containing object, the teacher, contributed to Andrea and Rosy's improvement. The skin sensations evoked by massage relieved Andrea's muscular tightening and brought particular memories of being vulnerable and not held closer to the surface, so that they were accessible to psychoanalytic exploration. Andrea's rigid breastfeeding posture, her rapid talking, and mastitis are seen here as a second skin used to avoid contact with her baby, who revived her uncontained primal experiences.

The touch experience with her baby enhanced the mother's tolerance for physical closeness by weakening her rigid defences. This occurred through Andrea's increasing awareness of her muscular tension and of its release through interactions with her baby. Such awareness was often accompanied by the emergence of memories and feelings in the psychoanalytic setting. As I wrote above, I highlight the significance of the presence of the teacher as a containing/reflective object to the mother's anxiety, and even more primitive states.

Talking about one of the first baby massage sessions, Andrea described the tension in her shoulders and arms preventing the massage movements from running smoothly: "I felt a blockage in my shoulders and chest, sometimes very painful and preventing me from breathing. It is an overwhelming sense of narrowness." I linked this to Andrea's stiff breastfeeding pose and the breast symptoms, and wondered whether she began developing this muscular tightening early in her life as a response to a lack of physical/emotional holding.

For the first time, Andrea was talking about her bodily experiences and feelings. She was not dealing with her body in abstract or idealized terms or as a stranger to herself. My objective was to lead her to an awareness of the link between her muscular tension and its emotional content. "Don't you think that this sense of held breathing is linked to the gesture of containment of the baby, in which chest and arms are mainly involved? Because you lacked the maternal containing gesture of chest and arms, you need now to adjust yours to your baby's primary needs', I said.

From then on, Andrea's enjoyment of baby massage increased over time. Rosy's achievement of mobility through massage had direct consequences, enabling her to elicit from her mother experiences of touch and handling that the mother had been lacking in her early life. Andrea was beginning to express a newfound liveliness, curiosity, and eagerness of interactions. These changes were made in the context of a positive relationship to me, which led Andrea to identify with me as someone who could enjoy playing with infants and who understood this in terms of transference (Andrea's relationship with her own mother and her relationship with her baby both being re-experienced with me).

I want to highlight an important process in psychotherapeutic work with parents and infants. When the mother has an inner space for rehearsal of her relations with her internal parents and thinking of these scenes in relation to her child, difficulties can be prevented. By resolving the conflicts with her own internal mother and father, she can free herself from them in her relationship with the baby, and find her own identity as a mother, according to the demands and needs of her individual baby.

Another important point is that the "change" in Andrea occurred because something was moving inside me as well. This mutual change allowed for a deeper understanding and connection, and was led by compassion and empathic perception.

Although the impact that clients can have on therapists is well known, mental health professionals are still taught early on to be on their guard for compassion and countertransference. They are warned of the negative potential of this for the client-therapist/ counsellor relationship and the risk of allowing oneself to get too close to a client's internal world and issues.

It is not well acknowledged that the client-counsellor/therapist relationship can also induce a powerful positive transformation in a therapist's own life and that this change is a powerful tool in the healing process.

The change induced by Andrea and Rosy in me redirected my life. I became increasingly aware of the importance of early support and my willingness to use my compassion and knowledge in this field.

The benefits experienced during the baby massage sessions came to be understood through the medium of analytic work as serving two functions. Firstly, the infant massage group helped Andrea to feel well held and to restore a sense of psychosomatic integration that had been seriously disrupted in her childhood. Secondly, the use of her own body to massage her baby enhanced her awareness of her muscular tension and its link with emotions. Baby massage offered her a context for restoring or keeping alive a sense of being well held and ease in her body. It also constituted a safe space where memories and feelings, which had been locked in the body since infancy, could be revived and become accessible to thought.

I want to examine the healing effect of the group itself. In a group, particular psychological phenomena occur. Bion (1948) had this intuition; he verified the therapeutic power of the group on individuals. In the individuals who form a group, specific tensions become manifest. In the sharing experience provided by the group, a parent can find a container in which she/he can voice or manifest her/his tensions and relieve them. Babies benefit enormously from the group as well. In a group special energy crosses the individual boundaries and a special time is created for both mothers and babies.

CHAPTER 6

An east/west approach to working with parents and infants and the healing relationship

This book presents a new perspective on health and the healing relationship, growing out of a meeting between Eastern meditative traditions and Western psychological practice. My regular practice of meditation and yoga helped me to heal Andrea's problem from within herself as well as within the relationship with her baby. I did not apply any therapeutic method but I was just led by "empathic perception" and "openness of the heart'. In our culture, the world "heart" has a rather sentimental meaning and is considered to be quite distinct from "mind", the latter usually referring to our rational and thinking capacity. In Eastern traditions, for instance in Buddhism, the world "heart" does not denote sentimental feelings, and the words "heart" and "mind" are part of the same reality ("citta" in Sanskrit). In fact, when Buddhists refer to mind, they point not to the head, but to the chest. This unity of mind and heart brings a fundamental openness and clarity, a much larger kind of awareness that resonates directly with the world around us.

Western psychology has been concerned about describing and analysing neurotic behaviour, and about developing therapeutic methods to help free people from conditioning. Western therapists know much less about how people can heal their neuroses from within. The weakness of Western modern health care resides in our ignorance about the sources of health inside us.

My aim was to work "with" Andrea on her past, not in a theoretical way but through her body, thus through her present feelings, and through her actual relationship with her baby. The capacity to let ourselves be touched in the heart by other people gives rise to expansive feelings of appreciation for others. I call this capacity "empathic perception', where heart connects with mind. When I suggested to Andrea she hold and hug her baby instead of fighting for not being able to breastfeed, I was "touched" by Rosy's state of abandonment and her slumped body. I was experiencing compassion, considered by Eastern traditions to be the noblest of human feelings.

During my work with Andrea and Rosy I was always illuminated by what I have learned from Eastern approaches to healing. I experienced moments of uncertainty about how to help Andrea and Rosy, but I used those moments to get a better sense for what was happening and get closer to them rather than summoning theory and technique. I drew on my own intuitive perception in responding to them and facing those moments of uncertainty. This is a new quality of "being with" mother and baby. The key is inside the therapist more than in theories. The moment of uncertainty is seen here not as threatening but as a source of intuition and creative possibilities. It allows for a new space of understanding, and higher attention.

Psychotherapy has mainly been concerned with the client's resistance to therapy, but has said little about the therapist's own resistance to greater openness. The most effective healing occurs when the therapist weakens her/his own resistance to get in "touch" with the client's fears and anxieties, thus to share the client's world.

Such a capacity to openness should concern not just psychotherapists but all professionals working with parents and infants. More than in any other area, the parent's fears, anxieties, and problems may often mirror unresolved issues in the therapist's or health professional's own life, related to birth and early experiences. I came to understand the midwives" resistance to be open to emotional issues related to Andrea's mastitis as defences against their anxieties related to their own primal experiences. Ironically, the midwives may have shared the same anxiety around contact as Andrea did towards her baby.

Real change brought about by therapy can only occur if I let myself experience what the client's reality feels like. True presence in therapists is possible when they let themselves be touched by the client, and when the client's feelings resonate inside them. I am speaking of true empathy and compassion. Real change in therapy occurs when we listen to our needs and feelings, rather than avoiding them.

During my work with Andrea I was often illuminated by Winnicott's work on the psyche-soma and other ideas from child development research and psychoanalysis, but those were continuously filtered by my feelings and intuition. The healing in clients is possible when they "feel" that the therapist provides a space in which they can explore and resolve their problems. The client can reach a larger awareness of the problem, allowing him/her to overcome it, rather than being stuck in it.

When the therapist trusts her/himself more than theory, this provides a model for how a client can begin to trust and connect with his or her own feelings and personal resources. When Andrea developed a mild mastitis after her second birth and the midwives were giving her antibiotics, she decided to use homeopathy and eventually became able to breastfeed. She had a new wisdom and confidence in her own feelings. Andrea was enabled to understand the function and meaning of her psychosomatic symptom and her use of her body, so that she could withdraw her destructive projections from her baby. With her third baby, she had no problems– at eight months she was still breastfeeding. She had gained a new awareness that emotions play an important part in breastfeeding and in labour. This new awareness led her to face labour with a quiet confidence in her own feelings, coming from reconciliation to her body.

Meditation can be of particular value for therapists or health professionals as it provides a practical way to learn to find trust in one's self. In Buddhism, this unconditional friendliness towards oneself is called "maitri'. The practice of meditation then, helps develop warmth and compassion towards our fears, insecurities, and emotional problems (entanglements), and open the heart. The therapist's acceptance of her/his own fears and insecurities helps the parent to face them, and in doing so he or she can face the client's own fears and help develop greater self-confidence.

Meditation shows how change is more dependent on how we "are" with ourselves than what we "do" to improve ourselves. Eastern meditation practices provide a comprehensive way of studying thought and emotion and developing compassion towards our own feelings and emotions and those of other humans. From my clinical experiences, I can say that meditation practice and yoga can bring enormous benefits to the healing relationship.

In exploring the "positive" value of a psychosomatic symptom in signalling to the therapist as well as to the client a need for change and healing, this book should prove useful not only to therapists and other health professionals but also to anyone interested in exploring the interrelationships between the psyche and the body, which means knowing more about ourselves.

What a symptom signifies

People who come to the psychotherapist are usually unaware of what they really suffer from. They complain about being depressed, having insomnia, being unhappy in their marriages, not enjoying their work, etc. They usually believe that their particular symptom is their problem and that their well-being depends on getting rid of it. A "cure', however, does not consist in removing symptoms, or in the absence of illness; but in the presence of well-being. Well-being is being in tune with the nature of human beings as a mind-body unity. This means to be open, receptive, sensitive, and aware–to become what one potentially is. It also means to be creative.

A baby needs her mother to be completely in tune with her true nature, which is an integrated body-mind, to be able to listen to her own feelings and become able to become a being in harmony with herself, thus to become creative. This state of complete attunement of the mother to the nature of the baby as well as to herself is what

Zen Buddhists call "enlightenment" or "satori" (Suzuki, 1949). It allows the mother to open all her senses and awareness, to connect with, and understand her baby. It enables the mother to "enjoy" the daily moments she shares with her baby.

In this book well-being is conceived in terms of a full union of mind and body, not in the negative meaning of the absence of sickness. During my work with Andrea and Rosy I never attempted to suppress the symptoms of mastitis, or the "faraway" quality of her language accompanied by a lack of eye contact, etc. My objective was to guide her to a new awareness or enlightenment, which would not have been possible without a complete transformation. A crucial moment in this "process" of intuition or enlightenment occurred when what had long been repressed began to be recovered into consciousness. Full recovery, however, was made possible by the simultaneous encouragement of the physical interactions between mother and baby, through the kangaroo method and baby massage. Baby massage proved a valuable place for insight, in which the mother did not feel judged or observed. Its playfulness allowed the mother to discover a new enjoyment of her baby.

Authentic psychoanalytic "insight" arrives without being forced. It is brought about not by theories or techniques, but by the therapist's feeling or intuition, which allows him or her to get in touch with the client's reality and thus to change it. Oriental psychology then can illuminate the analytic setting as well as sharpen the focus for a stronger insight.

I am grateful to the precious benefits of my regular practice of yoga and my interest in Eastern approaches to the healing relationship. I have found in much of the Buddhist teachings a universal, practical experience, much closer to me than many other Western theories.

A psychophysiological theory of emotion

The literature of Western psychology has conflicting theories about what emotion is, how it arises, and what it signifies. In Western culture emotions are treated as "other", separate from us. From

Plato onward the "passions" have usually been conceived as a sign of weakness. This is in contrast to an Eastern approach to healing, which considers that it is our alienation from emotions that makes them uncontrollable and a source of illness.

Either acting out or suppressing emotions reflect a dualistic attitude that only creates a split in us. We can clearly see this attitude in Andrea's case. When it comes to the mother-infant dyad, this split has detrimental consequences for the infant, who, in a mirroring process, will reflect the mother's separation and denial of emotions. We could see this effect on Rosy. The mother's emotions are vital nourishment for the infant and enable the infant to acknowledge her/his own emotions and deal with them constructively.

If we inhibit or suppress feelings or emotions because they seem overwhelming, our being will become fragmented and not a harmonious wholeness. They will become frozen and we become locked into them. This will be reflected in our posture, language, way of interacting, and other psychosomatic symptoms. This was particularly evident in Andrea's posture while breastfeeding, her "faraway" language, the lack of eye contact with her baby as well as with me, and mastitis.

It is interesting that the word "sad" has the same root as the word "satisfied', which means that it may be a kind of fullness of heart. Feeling sad often corresponds to a feeling of fullness in the heart, when the heart is "touched'. This fullness makes us fully alive and open to the world, unlike the frozen state of depression that alters our perception of the world and disconnects us from others. Again, we can see this in Andrea's disconnection with her baby.

By untangling Andrea's emotional problems, I aimed at a full access to a basic aliveness (or enjoyment of life), which, I believe is, fundamental nourishment for the infant's development. This was made possible by Andrea's acknowledgment of her suppressed emotions and their relationship to her muscular blockages. Emotions can indeed be inhibited by an excessive increase of muscular tension, which may have altered the breast muscle in Andrea and thus caused mastitis. It is also possible that the emotional stress may have altered the hypothalamic regulation of the secretion of hormones from the hypophysis. The hypothalamus is the control centre in the brain of primal activities, such as breastfeeding, and, through connections with the limbic system, of emotions.

Andrea also became aware of the impact of her suppressed anxiety and inhibited loving gestures towards her baby. A gesture in fact cannot be fully expressed if it is locked in by muscular/emotional tension. This led Andrea to increased bodyself awareness.

More than exploring the meaning of Andrea's feelings, I helped her face the emotional turmoil, in particular her anxiety around contact with her baby. My practice of meditation and yoga helped Andrea and I to work with emotions more directly and see them as a means for self-illumination or insight. Instead of perceiving emotions as a threat or judging them as good or bad, Andrea learned to accept them as they were.

No change is possible without working with emotions, as they are fluid expressions of our aliveness, and they are constantly changing. By facing her emotions directly, Andrea experienced the fullness of life. As something that touches us, emotion expresses the dynamic energy of life and can transmit great clarity. From my work experience and experience as a mother, I believe that an infant benefits enormously from sensing this fullness of life or pure aliveness in the parent. In fact this energy opens the parent's senses and heart (in the Eastern meaning), which connect them to the baby.

Andrea's overwhelming anxiety related to her primal experiences was aroused by contact with her baby. I never led her to building up thoughts about it, but to focus on her bodily feelings. I asked her what she had felt while breastfeeding or during labour, and the fact that she did not mention any physical sensation or feeling was a powerful indicator for both of us. The energy that I call fullness of life was locked in and prevented her from getting "in touch" with herself and thus with her baby. The point I want to make is that I was informed about that by experiences of her bodily feelings, not by her thoughts or interpretations of those experiences.

Over time Andrea learned that only by physically "feeling" her emotions fully could she open to herself and allow herself to discover their intelligence and communicative power. The anxiety she had been escaping became workable rather than taking her over.

My practice of yoga has influenced how I relate to myself, my clients, my family, and my work. Some knowledge about Buddhism has shown me that it is important to work with people in the "present', thus with the flow of their emotions, and not to cover up the situation with techniques learned while training. I worked with Andrea somatically. Working somatically does not necessarily mean bodywork, where I use my hands to manipulate connective tissues. I can also work with people's feelings, thoughts, gestures, and actions as expressions of the living body. It is important to pay attention to body language. This requires observational skills and the capacity to "listen" or to "be present". For instance, while observing Andrea's posture while breastfeeding (before she developed mastitis), I noticed some tension in her shoulders and stiffness throughout her body. On another occasion, I asked her what kind of information had come out of her feelings while breastfeeding. This kind of information is not cognitive. In fact she fled the answer and begun to talk about an idealistic breastfeeding, while her language had a distinct "faraway" quality, in that she sounded disconnected from her feelings and her whole somatic reality. This was a powerful source of information about her disturbed relationship to her bodyself.

It is interesting that the word "soma" from the Greek refers to the living body in its wholeness. Whatever we experience in and through the body forms our somatic reality, which includes feelings, emotions, thoughts, actions, symbols, sensations, and representations. When any of the expressions of the living body are suppressed, the wholeness and harmony of our somatic reality is undermined. And so is the psyche, as psyche and soma belong to each other.

When I work with parents and infants, I observe the parents" body language, listen to the sound of their bodies, and see how their primal experience has shaped their bodies, postures, breath, gestures, tone of voice, and ways of holding their babies. If there is tension in the holding of the baby or in the parent's tone of voice, I encourage the parent to focus on the muscular tension and its link to emotion.

If the *basic aliveness, joy of life*, or *"energy"* has been undermined by primal experiences, I try to gently encourage the unblocking of that energy. When this energy is blocked, the breathing does not unfold smoothly. This is particularly evident in a labouring woman. Her inability to let go, as a consequence of blocked energy, shows up as altered breathing. And breathing is a fundamental element in labour, during which it needs to expand in harmony with pelvic dilation, allowing the baby to be born. Andrea's breathing was narrowed by her screaming (upwards sounds instead of focused downwards sounds), and her fear of letting go. As a consequence, at some point during labour, her pelvis stopped dilating and the baby had to be taken out by ventous.

Labour and parenthood is a new and unknown experience for the first-time mother, yet it is coloured by the experience of her life in and through her body, which includes feelings, emotions, thoughts, cultural representations, sensations, and images.

Being present

The ability to be in the present moment is a major component of mental health. A baby needs her parents to be fully present for her healthy development, as by being present they can meet the baby's actual needs. The parents" perceptions of what is happening around them and the baby is often so altered by anxiety and apprehension that they can hardly see the individual baby. Much of their resources and energy are taken away by irrelevant worries and anxieties (either conscious or unconscious) about past experiences and future happenings.

A good therapist has "presence" and through mirroring teaches the parent to be fully present with the infant. Listening is a quality of being present. Very often questioning and listening are controlled by theories and technique, and may structure the answers. Talking in therapy can be a way of being in any other time and place except the present one. Helpful listening is just listening, a form of meditation, which provides the therapist with a direct experience of the client. Being present leads to a unity of therapist and client.

In Western society, our mind is constantly encouraged to be away from the present. We learn to be busy and do several things simultaneously. We are afraid of boredom. We are more concerned with becoming somebody rather then "being" someone. We are focused on doing things to achieve status and power. We build our self-image on the basis of actions rather than of a "being" that has an integrated psyche-soma.

We can feel when a person is "present" and is rooted, as she/he communicates her/his presence. This person is able to bring energy into what is happening all around him or her when it is happening. The ability to be in the present moment is a major component in therapy and any healing relationship, and determines its outcome. Now is the only time when we can actually do anything, when we can change. Focusing on "nowness" does not mean, however, overlooking the past and future but being aware of their interference in the present moment. When therapists are fully in the present, they can open all their senses and connect with the energy that flows in the client. But if they summon up theories, preconceptions, or techniques, the process of true understanding and "connection" cannot take place.

The sense of being present can commonly be seen in parents who attune with their baby. They seem to be rooted; to communicate a sense of dignity and respect in the present moment. All their energies are channelled to truly perceive what is happening around their baby. This can be evident to an attentive eye during a baby massage class. There is a clear difference between parents who massage their babies seeking to perform a task and those who play with the baby's experience. Being present with the baby means being attuned to him or her. Parents who feel present in their relationship with their baby experience an integration of mind and body, essential to sense the baby and meet his or her needs. This process is extremely important for the baby to learn to experience and know his or her true being.

The intimate sensorial and emotional connection with the developing baby can hardly unfold without the parents' ability to be attuned with their own feelings as well as with those of the baby. To establish the foundations of bonding it is of utmost importance to feel present to the infant experience. This feeling of rooted presence is needed from early pregnancy. Nevertheless, whether it is not strong primarily, there are some creative ways to help it blossom. For instance, a career woman who has decided to become a mother may find a hitch in dipping into this feeling of connection due to fear of an unknown experience. Conflicts are absolutely normal and are induced by pregnancy and the whole primal period. Denying and fleeing them is unhealthy. The crux is in finding a way to make them conscious and to constructively be with them.

Mindful baby massage and any creative time of contact such as playing music, singing, bathing, and the enjoyment of them, can enhance the sense of presence. The early pleasure experienced by the baby during massage (and indeed every time of attentive maternal contact), gradually sets the foundations for the child's ability to enjoy other experiences. I have heard mothers saying at the end of a baby massage session, "I feel so relaxed!" or, "It helps me banish thoughts from the mind." The playtime of baby massage, with games of touching, eye contact, vocalizing, smiling, combined with the containment of the group, can have healing effects on parent and baby.

In earliest life, no feelings or thoughts of the mother can be truly conveyed to the baby without the mediation of a lively body rooted in "nowness'. I speculate that the foetus senses the mother's feeling of presence in her experience of pregnancy and baby's life. The biological communication between mother and baby blossoms when the mother acknowledges the baby's sensitivity to her bodily cues. For instance, by laying the baby on her chest, with the baby's ear against her heart, rocked by her diaphragm in breathing, the mother allows the baby to rediscover the familiar beats he or she sensed in the womb. A baby lying in a crib untouched and unlistened to, however, is deprived of this biological dialogue.

This biological attunement requires from the mother a sense of "being present', attuned to her body/mind activities and language–breathing, muscle tone, emotions, feelings–and this sense of being present corresponds to psychosomatic integration and makes the experience with the child highly pleasurable.

Tension caused by worry or anxiety acts as a barrier, which hinders the parent's capacity to be present in the relationship with the baby. Conversely, the feeling of presence displays itself through a balanced muscular tone, evenly distributed through the body, an effectively functioning posture, self-confidence, and openness to listening. This results in wider receptiveness to the environment. We sometimes feel certain people have "presence', in that they seem to be rooted. Such a condition, i.e. the absence of barriers, allows the maternal creative energy to pass onto the baby.

Nurturing high expectations–for instance an ideal baby–can also act as a barrier to sensing the baby's needs and thus responding appropriately.

An open and mobile chest and relaxed shoulders (which deepens breathing and easily brings in a far greater volume of oxygen), conveys an attitude of "approachability" or 'listening'. In contrast, closed and stiff shoulders, with the chest locked and pulled inwards, are more likely to demonstrate an attitude of withdrawal or avoidance. The feeling of pleasure or enjoyment will induce an approach/forward posture whereas excessive anxiety, worry, and pain will induce an avoidance/backward posture. The iconic mother-child image has an open chest, containing arms, with the mother holding or breastfeeding her child, and both have an expression of pleasure.

When a baby cries, the mother commonly wonders why this is happening or whether something is wrong with her. If the mother's attempts to feed the baby are unsuccessful, this may give rise to anxiety. In more extreme cases, a persistent cry may generate a sense of guilt in the mother. This emotional state increases muscular tension and tightens the body. The baby senses this and, in a vicious circle, cannot cease crying. Communication breaks down. Thus the mother's tension and the baby's cries escalate until eventually the baby falls asleep very probably due to exhaustion. Wondering "why" while interacting with the baby may be worthless–it may be more helpful to attempt to sense the baby's body cues and movements. These will give the mother needed insights and guide her to find the appropriate response in a creative way.

Being in a hurry, away with her thoughts or worries, and so forcing the baby's tempo, increases the tension in both mother and baby and the synchronism between them is disrupted. The rhythm, which is a vital part of communication, alters. The tension, which is concentrated in parts of the body instead of being evenly distributed, prevents the mother's nurturing energy from flowing out. This deprives the baby as well as the mother of "total happening", as Winnicott says, or of integrated experiences. The experience of total happening is important in order to form a sense of integrated fulfilled identity and bodyself image, whilst the experience of "fragmentation" is at the basis of a split ego and bodyself.

Through the parental capacity to be present, to enjoy the journey into the primal period and the changes brought about by it, the baby learns to experience, enjoy, and know him or herself.

In this book, *pleasure* is not merely meant in terms of sensorial pleasure, but more importantly, in terms of the experience of integration and containment. The experience of pleasure denoted here involves respiratory, cardiac, and muscular changes, and results from the synthesis of sensory information with bodily of mental activities (Sansone, 2004, p. 101). Because of this synthesis, pleasure is an integrated experience of mind and body. There are immense benefits for a woman and her baby from enjoying her pregnancy and her relationship to her body. The mother's enjoyment and expression of her love are shown in the way she handles her baby in all the day-to-day details of maternal care (Abram 1996). Muscle tightening, as an expression of a second defensive skin, due to a primary skin impaired by a lack of containing experiences, diminishes such experiences of pleasure. Fear and anxiety have the same effects. In fact, muscular tension hinders the flow of information between body and mind and thus the integrated experience of pleasure.

Earliest enjoyment may shape the child's attitude to life and the ability to cope with stress through a true experience of self and his or her emotions. This attitude will help the child go through painful emotions by elaborating them with a constructive view rather than denying or suppressing them. Massage, for instance, can be an antidote to depression, or at least reduce the likelihood of developing depression in later life and can shape the child's attitude to disease.

The capacity to be present and listen does not concern just parents but also professionals, friends, or relatives who are offering support to the expectant or new parent. There is the mistaken belief that one is professional if he is able to "use" a certain technique, treatment, method, and so on. The effect of this belief can be detrimental in a healing or therapeutic relationship with parents or for a labouring woman. What a birthing woman needs, when there is no complication, is the support from midwife, partner, or friend, who is just "present". Being present does not necessary imply "doing", but "being with".

The following is a delightful account from a woman who gave birth to her three children with Michel Odent, the French pioneer of natural childbirth. A friend of hers, intrigued by the fact that she gave birth with the famous obstetrician, asked her how it was. The reply was, "Wonderful." Then she asked what he did and the privileged woman said, "Nothing–he spent all the time crouched in a corner".

The majority of birth professionals do not acknowledge the powerful effect of just "being present', which means summoning their own intuitions, feelings, and emotions. Rooted presence is conveyed through body language. Some of the most powerful channels are eye contact and a sympathetic smile. The woman's trust in a familiar presence is of utmost importance for a smooth labour and birth. The mother's ability to be present with the baby unfolds together with the reassuring feeling of being assisted in labour by a woman who is able to be present.

During labour a woman discovers basic primitive needs, for instance, the need for a present mother or mother figure, which is very different to the need for medical intervention. To be able to mother, a woman needs to be mothered. A doula is a familiar figure in labour–a woman who plays the role of mother–just by her supportive presence. One study (Wolman, Chalmers, Hofmeyr, & Nikodem, 1993) showed that doula-assisted mothers developed a relationship with their babies much more quickly and smoothly than the non-supported mothers, and picked up their babies more frequently. Doula-assisted mothers also perceived themselves as closer to their babies, as managing better, and as communicating better with their babies than the control group mothers. I believe emotional support is an essential ingredient for every labouring woman. It is needed not only to improve the obstetric outcomes but also the special relationship that ties the parents to their infants. A most important aspect of emotional support in childbirth is that of the calm, accepting, and holding model provided for the parent.

Research (Sauls, 2002) provides powerful evidence of improved outcomes for mothers and babies when mothers are emotionally supported in labour. These outcomes include, but are not limited to: lower rates of analgesia and anaesthesia use, lower operative birth rates, shorter labour, as well as increased maternal satisfaction with the birthing process and their baby.

During my study of pregnant women I found out how important it is for most women to see a familiar figure on a regular basis throughout their pregnancy and beyond. They need an experience of continuity, while the shift system for midwives means that some women meet their midwife in labour for the first time.

For an expectant father, being present in labour may mean being silent but present in the birth room, or if she needs it, being actively involved in massaging the woman's back, breathing deeply with her, supporting her from her armpits, or simply holding her hand. It may also mean being in the next room. Getting in tune with the labouring woman's needs means perceiving and understanding her body language–facial expressions, eye contact, voice, and gestures. If her partner feels overwhelmed by anxiety or fear, this could make it difficult to read the woman's non-verbal cues. In this case, it is better to stay in a corner and not intervene. Or if the father's anxiety begins to tighten the surrounding energy, he can be equally present while staying in the next room.

When I was in labour, I experienced the midwives "monitoring" of my baby's heart at regular intervals like an intrusion. Fortunately, my labour and birth were complication-free, but even the thought of receiving medical intervention made me feel how intrusive it would have been. I only needed someone's quiet presence.

In working with parents and infants, any intervention with techniques or theories could be perceived by parents and/or infants as intrusive and lead the therapist or health professionals far away from the client's real needs and feelings.

CHAPTER 7

Emotions and the primal brain

There is no such thing as an infant...without maternal care there would
be no infant.   (Winnicott, 1960b, p. 39)

Neurobiological studies show that healthy brains depend on healthy
bonding relationships with the primary caregivers and efficient
connections of neurons in the brain. All these connections make
the brain of a two-year-old four times heavier than the newborn's.
Early events determine which circuits in the brain will be reinforced
and maintained. It is the emotional environment in particular that
reinforces this wiring system and determines the density and
complexity of connections among the neurons. Neurobiologists
show us that the wiring is related to the quality of the parent-infant
relationship, the way the baby is cared for, and the quality of the
baby's attachment to the parents and others.

Development is about incorporating experience into the
developing brain, thus producing new connections and reinforcing
them. The capacity of the brain to modify its own structure in
response to the environment is called neuroplasticity. Perry,
Pollard, Brakely, Baker, & Vigilante have stated (1995): "The single

most significant distinguishing feature of all nervous tissue–of neurons–is that they are designed to change in response to external signals. Those molecular changes permit the storage of information by neurons and neural systems."

During the first few years of life the brain is most open to being influenced and during this time necessary connections are formed and reinforced. This is why early intervention is most beneficial.

Physiologically, the human baby is still very much part of the mother's body. He or she depends on her milk for food and to provide immune protection. The mother's touch regulates the baby's muscular activity and hormone levels. Her feeding and touch disperse the baby's stress hormones. The baby's life depends on this basic physiological regulation.

To respond to the baby's needs and feelings, the mother has to identify with them in such a way that the baby's needs feel like hers. By responding to the baby's feelings in a non-verbal way, the mother regulates the baby's physiological and psychological states. She does this mainly with her facial expressions, her tone of voice, her smell, and her touch. She gets her baby's crying to a calmer state by using a soothing voice, or by holding and rocking him. She gets the baby into a state in which the baby feels comfortable again.

Caregivers who cannot feel attuned to their baby, because they find it difficult to be in touch with, and regulate, their own feelings, will pass their regulatory problems onto their baby. Such a baby cannot learn how to monitor his or her own states and adjust them effectively from a mirroring process. He or she will probably never know his or her feelings, or will repress them, since the parents did not notice them or were not interested in them. However, if parents do understand the baby's states and respond quickly to them, restoring a feeling of comfort, then feelings can come to awareness. The baby will learn to expect the parents' responses to acquire patterns. These non-verbal patterns, unconsciously acquired, were named by John Bowlby (1969) "internal working models". He suggested that feelings are conveyed through facial expressions, posture, tone of voice, physiological changes, and tempo of movement.

The expectations of our parents and other meaningful people are stored in our brain during our infancy. They become models that monitor our behaviour in relationships throughout life. This process occurs without our conscious awareness.

The parent therefore helps the baby to become aware of his or her own feelings through mirroring, for instance by talking in baby talk and emphasising his or her sounds, words, and gestures so that the baby can become aware of them (Gergely & Watson, 1996). It is through this process of identification of feelings and mirroring that the baby learns to regulate his or her emotions and is introduced to human culture.

If, however, the caregiver tends to inhibit his or her own feelings due to an uncomfortable relationship with them, he or she is unlikely to identify with the baby's feelings. If he or she is preoccupied with unresolved emotional issues, she may not notice the baby's feelings, regulate them, or define them. This process also shapes the child's capacity to feel empathy, which derives from being able to identify his or her own feelings while at the same time identifying those of other people.

Good relationships depend on this capacity, especially on being able to tolerate uncomfortable feelings. If the caregiver has not learnt how to monitor "negative" states like anger and hostility, he or she will tend to hold back or suppress such feelings, and will find them very hard to manage in his or her child. The child will learn to suppress such feelings. This is what would have probably happened to baby Rosy without my early support. The mother's concerns and anxieties were taking her away from her own feelings as well as from Rosy's, and the process of identification and mirroring were not taking place effectively.

The child's ability to know his own feelings, thanks to the parent's ability to monitor them, will allow him or her to develop a strongly integrated psyche-soma and bodyself, and to understand others and relate to them with confidence.

Insecure attachments therefore jeopardise the baby's nervous system. Inappropriate or disattuned parental responses actually disturb the baby's natural rhythms. An intense emotional state normally generates a physiological arousal that will lead to action, and then once the feeling has been expressed, the organism will return to normal. If the arousal level is not brought down, however, the cycle remains uncompleted, with consequent disturbances such as muscle tension, held breathing, hormonal, or immune disturbances. Even if feelings are suppressed, the cardiovascular system, in particular, will remain activated (Gross & Levenson, 1997).

A baby eventually learns to regulate itself, but for a long time depends on its parents to regulate its states of body and mind. Healthy functioning depends on the internal symphony of balanced fluctuation of inhibitory and excitatory activity.

The capacity to understand another person's state is learnt in infancy from our earliest caregivers, usually our parents. This capacity enables individuals to adjust smoothly to each other's needs and thus to have comfortable intimate relationships. This effective exchange of emotional cues within a relationship is called by Tiffany Field "psychobiological attunement" (Field, 1985). To be attuned to another individual's needs, however, we need to be attuned to our own internal states. In order to act effectively, we need to be able to read the emotional information provided by our bodies (Fig 2).

Fig. 2. Mutually synchronised interactions are fundamental to the child's affective development (special attunement between father and child).

Children who have developed insecure attachments have not learnt effective strategies to deal with their emotions. They cannot cope with their feelings and so cannot reflect upon them. When feelings are used as valuable signals for both the state of our own organism as well as that of others, then we can create a culture in which the feelings of others are important, respected, and responded to.

To maintain relationships we need to monitor other people as well as our own internal state, noticing feeling signals and body language. Babies are very good at this–even as newborns they are highly responsive to other humans' facial expressions and tones of voice. If we watch parents and babies interacting, we see them performing a dance. The parent's facial expressions will be important for the child's cues on how to behave when they begin to experiment with their growing independence.

I suggest that the baby's capacity for self-regulation can benefit from regular mindful massage. The natural sensory stimulation of massage speeds up myelination of the brain and the nervous system. The myelin layer is a fatty covering that encases each nerve. It protects the nervous system and speeds the transmission of impulses from the brain to the rest of the body. The process of encasing the nerves is not complete at birth; stimulation speeds the process, thus improving brain-body communication. In psychological terms, this enhances integration between mental and bodily processes and therefore the integration of the bodyself image.

The parts of the brain beneath the cortex, the *brainstem*, and the *hypothalamus* are involved in the body's self-regulation, in emotion and communication. The cranial nerves are initially involved in self-regulation of visceral functions, such as circulation of the blood, breathing, eating, and digestion. Vocalization, speech, and facial expressions are produced through muscle systems that are controlled by the cranial nerves. We can then see the relationship between emotions, muscle systems, and visceral functions and how they are involved in relationships and communication. The baby is born with a vital need to have these systems nurtured by mindful sensory stimulation. Skin contact, sensitive touch, and eye contact strengthen the relationship and integration between emotions, muscle systems, and visceral functions (Sansone, 2004).

The cranial nervous system, in particular the brainstem and the hypothalamus, are also involved in the development of the bodyself image. This system is well formed, even in a seven-week-old human embryo, long before the cerebral cortex has even begun to form. Studies on embryos' brains (Trevarthen, 2003) indicate that the *emotional system* or the brainstem/hypothalamus self-regulatory system monitors cortical development. This process continues throughout life. This system controls attention, muscle tone, and motor activity. Emotional systems thus influence cognitive and behavioural development and also language, contrary to some theories that it is the other way round. Attuned parental responses to the infant's needs and feelings allow the primal emotional systems to develop harmoniously. From them, all the other systems, language, cognitive, and social behaviour will unfold in synchrony.

Interaction and the Social Brain

Babies are born with the capacity to relate to others and to learn, but they need caregivers, usually the parents, who let this capacity unfold. Colwyn Trevarthen (2001b) contends that babies are born with innate regulatory capacities that motivate them to engage in relationships. He stresses the fundamental role of emotion and relationships in the infant's development. Even a premature baby can interact in rhythmic "proto-conversational" patterns in time with the vocalizations, touches, and expressions of face or hands, of an attentive and affectionate adult (Trevarthen, 1999, 2001a; Trevarthen, Kokkinaki, & Fiamenghi, 1999; Van Rees & de Leeuw, 1987).

Trevarthen's study of communicative and cooperative exchanges between infants and adults brought about radical change, undermining the reductive cognitive perspective and classic psychoanalytic models. Since the late 1970s, he has conducted research that reviews the very young baby's emotional, communicative, and relational capacities. In contrast to the idea of babies as unskilled, Trevarthen has shed light on the baby's innate musical intelligence, narrative awareness, and capacity to engage in relationships.

Accurate observations are an invaluable resource in conjunction with theory, and illustrate, for example, how skilled and powerful infants are as active contributors in a relationship. Babies have an innate predisposition to use the mother and objects around them to satisfy their need to explore and perceive. Babies brains, as studies on foetuses and newborns show (Yamada et al, 2000; Trevarthen, 2001a, 2001b), are organized in a way that makes them prone to relating to others. However, to develop this predisposition, infants need a relationship–the mother's body–that provides an environment for their earliest experiences.

Klein (1948) describes the infant's innate curiosity in exploring the mother's body–the instinct for knowledge. Bion (1962) highlights the baby's need for interaction with the mother to experience itself. Stern (2000) refers to a core self or an innate core self-image. It seems likely that the baby is born with a prior image of the mother's existence, developed during intra-uterine life through the mother's feelings and thoughts. Before the baby can see, the baby is seeing.

Research (Bruner, 1983; Trevarthen, 1999; Trevarthen, 2002) points to the conclusion that the foundation for interpersonal communication–verbal, gestural, and postural–is present at birth and likely to be present before birth. It consists in the games that mother and baby play with their body language.

Relatedness is acquired in the uterus and this is indicated by the neonate's recognition of his or her mother's voice, smell, and touch, as can be demonstrated by the infant's capacity to orientate towards her. The baby is born fully equipped physically and emotionally to handle the brain wiring and social interactions. The most vital source of nourishment for the baby's brain is the emotional environment.

> The ecological niche to which the baby has evolved the ability to adapt is the relationship with the mother. Research suggests that emotion operates as a central organising process within the brain. In this way, an individual's abilities to organise emotions–a product in part of earlier attachment relationships–directly shapes the ability of the mind to integrate experience and to adapt to future stressors, [Seigal, 1999, p. 4].

Turner suggests that "our ability to be so emotional" is the foundation of our rationality and our language abilities (Turner, 2000, p. 60).

The *prefrontal* part of the cortex has the unique role of linking the sensory areas of the cortex with the emotional and survival-oriented subcortex. The *orbitofrontal* cortex (behind the eyes, next to the amygdala and cingulate), which is the first part of this prefrontal, plays a key role in emotional life (Fig 3).

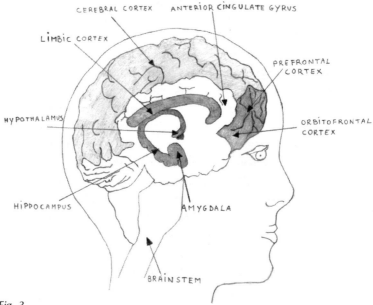

Fig. 3.

Neuroscientists have showed that if the prefrontal area is impaired, social life is undermined. This area, together with other parts of the prefrontal cortex and anterior cingulate, is responsible for "emotional intelligence", as Daniel Goleman calls it (Goleman, 1996). The orbitofrontal cortex is responsible for the capacity to empathise, i.e. to feel to some degree what others feel.

Allan Schore considers the orbitofrontal cortex the controller for the entire right brain, which is dominant in earliest life (Schore, 2003a). It is also responsible for our emotional memory and aesthetic experiences such as the flavour of food, the pleasure of touch, and the recognition of beauty (Rolls, 1999).

The orbitofrontal cortex is involved in recognising other people's emotional cues and thus responding accordingly. It plays a major role in controlling our emotional responses, as it is connected to the subcortical basic emotional systems (lymbic system, amygdala, and hypothalamus). These systems can be activated or inhibited by the prefrontal cortex, according to social circumstances and what is socially acceptable. The orbitofrontal cortex can therefore suppress impulses and feelings arising in the subcortical areas. However, the orbitofrontal areas can only be tuned to the deeper systems of the brain while they are activated. It is a mediator between cortex and subcortex.

What is particularly interesting in the context of psychotherapeutic work with parents and infants is that the orbitofrontal cortex begins to develop in our earliest relationships and within the first three years of life. It is unlikely to develop well without experiences with a caring adult. It is very plastic and can learn to adapt to whatever culture, family, and circumstances the child finds itself in.

A baby's developing orbitofrontal area, like the whole brain, is damaged when exposed to neglect, trauma, or prolonged maternal depression.

> For even though the child will never remember the specific events at any conscious level, his lower limbic system–and the amygdala in particular–does store powerful associations between an emotional state, life fear, or pain, and the person or situation that brought it on. Associations may be indelible. [Eliot, 2001]

Seigal (1999) stated "human connections shape the neural connections from which the mind emerges." Therefore the social capacities of the brain develop in response to social experiences with a caring adult and are closely correlated to early emotions. When the child is deprived of social relationships during the first three years of life (a critical period in which the orbitofrontal areas normally develop), it is very unlikely to recuperate these lost social abilities or develop this part of the brain well. This is why early support is highly important.

An important promoter of social interaction in the baby is making it "pleasurable". To simply lovingly hold the baby and enjoy it is the most powerful trigger of brain development. When a mother is finding pleasure in her relationship with her baby, she is contributing to the development of the baby's prefrontal cortex and his or her capacity for self-regulation, monitoring of emotions, and social interactions.

If, however, the mother's capacity to enjoy her baby is impaired by severe difficulties then the baby's development is jeopardised. This is why early support can bring enormous benefits to the mother-baby system. For the baby, being held, touched, and talked to with love are the most powerful spurs to development, even more than breastfeeding. I constantly suggested this to Andrea during my work with her and her baby. Touched by her baby's state of deprivation of contact, and by Andrea's struggling with herself for not being able to give her baby her milk, one day I turned to Andrea saying that her baby needed her presence, love, holding, and touching even more than her breastmilk.

Enjoyment is a psychophysiological condition in which the muscles relax and breathing can deepen, so that gentle stroking or calm rocking can occur. I equal this condition to being "fully present". When the baby is in his or her mother's or father's arms, which reflect the parent's sensation of pleasure, his or her tensions and fears are dispersed, muscles can relax and breathing can be smoothened, bringing on a feeling of safety and warmth. Now the baby is mirroring the parent's pleasurable experience– her/his state of relaxation.

The baby's heart rate synchronizes with the parent's heart rate. Through touch, the mother communicates her love, and soothes the baby. Her love and touch are a reflection of her autonomic nervous system, which communicates with her baby's nervous system. There is a "psychophysiological" attunement between mother and baby.

Through smell, touch, and sound the baby receives his or her first sources of pleasure. Touch and sound are already powerful sources of pleasure in the womb. In fact the baby already recognises his or her mother from her voice, touch, and smell.

The power of eye contact and body language

Eye contact is a powerful element that helps establish the bonding between parent and infant. Other important elements are skin contact, the parents' voice, and baby's response to it, smell, rhythms of communication, activation of maternal hormones by contact with the baby, and temperature regulation.

Internal states can be completely visible in our face, gestures, movements, and posture. Emotions vibrate through our body and can be sensed as well as seen (Sansone, 2004). Particularly sensitive to vibrations, the baby senses the caregiver's mental and emotional state through the way in which he or she is held, touched, talked to, and looked at. Observing face-to-face communication between mother and baby, Trevarthen (2001b) notes that proto-conversation is mediated by eye contact, vocalizations, hand gestures, and movements of the arms and head, all acting in coordination to express interpersonal awareness and emotions. He indicates that the development of the infant's brain requires brain-to-brain interaction and occurs in the context of an intimate and positive affective relationship. In other words, it is the caregiver's emotional availability and consistent bodily expressions that seem to be the most central feature of early experience in promoting development.

Eye contact is one of the most powerful channels of communication at our disposal, and it strengthens the connection between parent and infant. The baby's visual system is biologically programmed to seek out the mother's eyes. Eye contact may be a powerful cue for the infant's physiological system; it sends signals to the brain that allow it to reduce the production of stress hormones initiated during childbirth.

Researchers examined what happened when a mother was asked to maintain an unchanging, neutral expression and to be unresponsive to her three-month-old baby's signals (Tronik, Als, Adamson, Wisu, & Brazelton, 1978). Initially, the baby tried to elicit the mother's attention. After a few minutes, the baby began to fuss and cry and became irritable. If a mother is sad for several days, her baby will become distressed and irritable. This mother transfers her emotions to her baby through a facial expression of sadness and is less sensitive and responsive to her. Eye contact is the main source of information about other people's feelings and intentions; feelings are seen on the face.

Eye contact can release strong positive feelings. When the infant looks at her mother, the mother feels much closer to her (Fig. 4). The psychoanalyst Fraiberg (1974) has described in detail the difficulties that parents of blind infants have in feeling close to them. Without the mutual gazing, parents feel lost and like strangers to their babies until both learn to substitute other means of communication for this. Newborn babies find eyes particularly engrossing. Certainly attentiveness to faces is hard-wired into human beings and is evident even in newborns.

Fig. 4. In infancy, smile, eye contact and positive looks, conveying positive feelings, help baby's brain grow.

By toddlerhood, the child has started to use the mother's and the father's faces as immediate guides to behaviour in his environment. The child will use visual communication at a distance to check out what to do and what not to do, what to feel and what not to feel, using the parent's facial expressions as the source of information (Feinman, 1992). The quality of the earliest eye contact between parent and baby affects the baby's capacity to relate to others. While observing the behaviour of children over five months old in mother-and-baby classes, I saw how the mothers' presence and eye contact allowed them to feel secure and explore the space around them, to interact with other children and therefore to experience themselves.

I can describe a case demonstrating the importance of eye contact in affecting an infant's growth. When I worked at the University Hospital in Rome I saw a four-and-a-half month-old child who came to hospital because her parents were concerned about her lack of responsiveness, delayed development, and low weight. She also had strabismus. The parents were convinced that her strabismus might result from a brain abnormality. When I observed the mother and the baby interacting, I noticed they never made eye contact. When I asked about this, the mother said, "I don't know which eye she is using, so I have stopped trying to look at her eye-to-eye." After surgery on the deviating eye, when the baby's eyes could move together normally, a remarkable change occurred in the mother-baby interaction, with more smiling and responsiveness. By one year of age, the baby had gained weight and was showing a normal rate of growth.

According to Allan Schore (1994), in infancy eye contact and smiles help the brain to grow. Shore suggests that it is positive looks that are the most vital stimulus for the growth of the social, emotionally intelligent brain. It has been observed that the pupil of the eye acts as a tool of non-verbal communication (Hess, 1975). When the baby looks at his or her caregiver and sees dilated pupils, the baby receives information that the caregiver's sympathetic nervous system is aroused, and is experiencing pleasure. In response, the baby's own nervous system becomes pleasurably aroused and the heart rate increases. There is a biochemical attunement between caregiver and baby. When pleasure is experienced, the neuropeptide beta-endorphin is released into the blood–specifically into the orbitofrontal region of the brain. Beta-endorphin is known to help neurons grow by regulating glucose and insulin (Shore, 1994). Beta-endorphin is a natural opiod that is responsible for feeling good. At the same time, another neurotransmitter, dopamine, is released from the brainstem and reaches the prefrontal cortex. Dopamine has an energising and stimulating effect. Therefore eye contact and smiles, conveying positive feelings, contribute to the growth of the social brain (Shore, 1994). It seems that the amount and quality of neuronal connections depend on the infant having positive experiences. With a more richly networked brain, the child is able to use the brain more effectively and to perform better.

The synaptic connections in the prefrontal cortex reach their highest density just when attachment and bonding are particularly strong, between six and twelve months. It is also when the parent-child relationship becomes highly pleasurable.

In my work with mothers and babies, I have found that the mother's smile, as an expression of a pleasurable relationship with her baby, is a great spur to development. When Andrea smiled at her baby Rosy for the first time, a "sensitive contact" was being made. Then she picked up the baby and Rosy gazed at her mother and emitted some vocalizations for the first time. It really seemed that Andrea was meeting her baby for the first time. After this turning point, I saw Andrea increasingly interact with the little girl during the next three visits. After nine visits, this mother-baby "meeting" gave me the first opportunity to see Rosy in an alert state. She also gained in liveliness and physical vigour. This is only one example of how sensitive interactions (such as smiling, attuned touching, and holding), the first sources of pleasure, are the most important triggers of attachment/bonding and growth.

In Andrea, the breastfeeding experience as well as the capacity to enjoy her baby were both initially undermined by her emotional difficulties. One of the most significant changes in the relationship between Andrea and Rosy was the mother's capacity to "enjoy" holding her baby. It is interesting that oxytocin is both the hormone responsible for milk let down *and* the hormone of pleasure.

Many parents may not realise that their facial expressions, eye contact, smile, touching, tone of voice, holding, and mimicking are vital spurs in their child's development. Supportive or therapeutic work with parents and infants cannot overlook ongoing parent-baby interactions made up of these vital elements. Any kind of work that overlooks these concrete interactions takes a parent further away from the baby's experience.

How the brain matures in terms of social and psychological development–the most complex levels of human functioning–begins in early life through an evolving relationship with these bodily rhythms of communication.

Internal patterns

Our social intelligence is largely shaped by the experiences we have between six and eighteen months. When associations between neurons are formed into patterns, the baby begins to categorize his/her experiences with other people on the basis of expectations. The baby will store how the person's face looked, and the feeling he or she had in her body during that experience. The repetitiveness of experiences form emotional patterns in the brain as stored images, which act as predictors. These inner images function as a social reference–a guide to interaction.

Experiences that are particularly threatening or arousing are registered in the amygdala and will provoke an instant response to it. Happily, positive social interaction with others can inhibit the amygdala's responses to situations of danger, thus repairing early fear conditioning. The prefrontal area and anterior cingulate are responsible for conscious self-awareness and allow an individual to revise the earlier patterns under new circumstances. The individual becomes able to reflect upon experiences and consider options before taking action. The prefrontal cortex has strong connections with not only the subcortical emotional systems (including the hypothalamus and the amygdala), but also the sensory system conveying information about the outside world, as well as the motor areas of the brain and its chemical activities. With all this information, the prefrontal cortex can monitor the overall state of the organism.

The internalized parental images become an important source of emotional self-regulation. If the parents teach the child affective strategies for soothing and calming high arousal, the child is more likely able to monitor his or her emotions and cope with stress.

As I have described, smiling and positive facial expressions are stored and become an important spur to development. Negative looks and interactions are also stored and can trigger a biochemical response, just as the positive facial expressions do. The parent's disapproving face can trigger stress hormones such as cortisol, just as a smile or positive look induces pleasurable feelings by activating endorphins and dopamine neurons.

Parental facial expressions have a powerful impact on the child, as the child uses them to regulate his or her physiological and psychological states. In my book *Mothers, Babies and their Body Language* I describe how the child organizes his or her muscle tension and posture as a repetitive response to the parent's looks, holding, touching, tone of voice, and posture. These expressions of body language induce in the child a muscle tension response that is stored in the muscle and overall body. In the long term this forms muscle memory and posture (Sansone, 2004).

As Schore (1994) explains, a toddler's brain also needs a certain amount of cortisol for development. This is important in helping the orbitofrontal cortex inhibit emotional arousal, by forming connections with the parasympathetic nervous system (via the hypothalamus). The parasympathetic system is the inhibitory system, very important for the child's growth, as it enables the child to understand when behaviour is acceptable or dangerous, and to stop if appropriate. This capacity allows the child to fit into a social group and culture. The child needs the parents to bring the level of arousal down and restore regulation, otherwise he or she may remain locked in a state of arousal.

From body language to verbal language

The right brain is dominant in the earliest months of the child's life. Once the child has acquired the ability to manage feelings with the development of the orbitofrontal cortex, the right and left sides of the orbitofrontal cortex become highly connected. The left brain starts to play a major role, and specializes in analytical and verbal processing, unlike the right brain's intuitive ability to form a broader picture. It seems that the left brain monitors the organized self that has been shaped by the right brain's activities, and conveys this self to other people.

At this final stage of early emotional development of the brain, when the verbal self emerges, the brain becomes less open to change. This is why early psychotherapeutic work with parents and infants is particularly beneficial. This also explains why I believe in prevention more than in cure. It is much easier to bring about changes to parent-infant interactions, and thus correct a child's difficulties, than to heal an adult's problems or mental illness.

As I have described, the development of the right brain, in particular of the orbitofrontal cortex, occurs at a crucial time in infancy and depends on our earliest relationships. Our verbal skills and our verbal self emerge from the right brain, in other terms, from all those psychophysiological rhythmic exchanges between parent and infant. Evidence now clearly indicates that these earliest emotional non-verbal interactions affect the development of the infant's consciousness and verbal development (Trevarthen, 2001b; Trevarthen, 2002).

New areas of the brain, the anterior cingulate and hypothalamus, now begin to develop. The child develops a greater awareness of feelings and of inner states, such as pain and pleasure. With the development of the dorsolateral cortex, the child becomes able to develop memories and thoughts. The child can now plan, think about experiences, and make choices.

In the second year linguistic ability develops. As the dorsolateral cortex and the anterior cingulate develop, emotions can be communicated through words as well as through touch and body language. Rather than relying on automatic associations of past experiences, based on feedback from people's facial expressions and body language, the child can now reflect upon alternative solutions. However, the child continues to use non-verbal body language as a reference for his or her emotional responses.

If the parents are attuned to the child's emotional state and can talk about it, and thus symbolise it in words, the child is likely to be able to express feelings and differentiate between them. Talking about feelings to others is an effective way of monitoring emotional arousal, as the child can rely on new feedback and reflection.

The hippocampus, which also develops in the third year, receives and synthesises sensory information, giving it a time and a place. The hippocampus is responsible for remembering where and when particular personal events happened. It is closely linked to the anterior cingulate and the dorsolateral prefrontal cortex. Significant events are remembered now in sequence and the child becomes aware of a past and a future. This enables the child to develop a narrative self, a self who does not live solely in the present moment. Parents can now recall the past to the child–"Do you remember when we went to Mary's party?"–or express their plan to the child, "Tomorrow we're going to the beach."

The left brain (in particular the dorsolateral prefrontal cortex, anterior cingulate, and hippocampus) plays a major role in the development of a social self, a self who has an autobiographical memory and who communicates with others verbally. However, our social self and our verbal capacities emerge from the deeper right brain or emotional abilities. Emotional health depends very much on effective connections between the left brain and right brain and on their integrated work. When the two brain hemispheres work together harmoniously, the child has more possibilities for reflecting upon emotions, to express them effectively, and thus to monitor them. The child has more communicative resources and a secure sense of self. Caring, attentive earliest relationships encourage healthy/integrative functioning of the left and right brain.

As I have described, emotional health depends on psychosomatic integration. From a neuropsychological perspective, this corresponds to the integration of left- and right-brain functions, which means that all the brain functions work harmoniously. This is only possible when the child receives attuned interactions and experiences positive bonding and secure attachment.

Certainly, when emotions are blocked from awareness, because they have not been acknowledged or identified, or have been neglected or denied, the child will be less able to reflect on them using the left-brain resources.

In Andrea there was an inability to verbalize or symbolise her feelings, thus to use the left-brain's reflective and narrative capacities. In fact, she had missed the earliest attentive relationships and positive feedback from her parents, which would have been important in enabling her to acknowledge her feelings and put them into words. These abilities can only develop as a result of the integration of all the functions of the brain.

Attachment and the stress-coping-system

Mutually synchronized interactions are fundamental to the infant's ongoing affective development. If attachment is an interactive psychobiological synchrony, stress is defined as an *asynchrony* in a sequence of interactions. However, a period of re-established synchrony allows for stress recovery. The key to this is in the mother's capacity to monitor and regulate her own emotions, especially negative emotions. A fundamental function of attachment is to promote the regulation or synchrony of biological and behavioural systems within the organism. Mutual synchronization of physiological rhythms is an essential process that mediates attachment formation (Schore, 1994, 2000a, 2000b). In other words, in an attachment bond, the mother is attuning and resonating with the rhythms of the infant's internal states and then regulating the arousal level of these positive and negative states. Attachment therefore concerns the regulation of emotional states, aimed at minimizing negative emotions and facilitating opportunities for positive emotions. An early relationship and attachment bond are internal processes that shape the infant's nervous system and all the psychobiological systems. These systems require interaction with the environment to establish networks and mature. Evidence now clearly indicates that these earliest emotional non-verbal interactions also affect the development of the infant's consciousness and verbal development (Trevarthen, 2001b; Trevarthen, 2002). I equate such a complex and coherent organization of the brain with an integrated bodyself.

All adults can experience infantile feelings of helplessness, bringing back echoes of not being held and asynchronized communication. In extreme therapeutic settings, this can lead the patient to holding him or herself together. The same may happen to a new mother and father whose baby arouses their primary feelings of not being held. At first, these survival measures are adaptive. Gradually these defence mechanisms can structure the character, if they are not followed by re-established synchrony that allows for stress recovery. Some will lead to socially adaptive behaviour and special abilities; others can block emotional development and lead to disintegration of posture and motility on the one hand, and of communication, behaviour, and abilities on the other.

I should emphasise the difference between "non-integration", which is a passive experience of non-containment, and "disintegration", an active defensive splitting process in the service of development. The baby's attempts to hold herself together when distressed are no different from the adaptive mechanism used at times of crisis when an adult experiences non-integration.

Behaviour in a patient, such as refusing to speak, holding back from expressing feelings, muscle tightening and postural stiffening, constant talking, jumping from one subject to another, or being busy all the time, can be seen as defensive attitudes, attempts to hold the self and the body together. We can see some of these behaviours in Andrea. In psychotherapy, they oppose the analytic relationship, yet they express the patient's need to hold him or herself together and his or her fragility. The analyst thus may feel rejected by the patient. The analyst's feeling of rejection can lead the patient to reinforce the defence mechanisms, as he or she holds on to these primitive anxieties and feels that nobody is being understanding. Only a therapist who understands the defensive function of the patient's behaviour and helps the patient through the transitory states of non-integration, rebirth, and primary dependence on the maternal object can strengthen this internal fragility. The therapeutic setting therefore becomes the containing object.

Studies of attuned communication (Schore, 1994) between an empathic mother and her baby indicate that the emotional synchrony is exquisitely non-verbal and that this is a *resonance* that is more than just between her psychobiological states and the baby's mental states. The mother also acts as a regulator of the infant's physiology. Psychotherapeutic work with parents, or parents-to-be, and infants thus implies the therapist's capacity to *attune* to the parent's psychophysiological state, acting as a regulator of his or her physiology (Lyons-Ruth, 2000).

The right hemisphere seems to be, more than the left, primarily involved in the psychophysiological attunement between mother and baby. The right hemisphere is, more than the left, deeply connected not only with the limbic system (particularly involved in emotion) but also with both the sympathetic and the parasympathetic branches of the autonomic nervous system. Therefore, the representation of visceral and body states is predominantly under the control of the non-dominant hemisphere. The right cerebral cortex rather than the left seems to be the site of an integrated map of the bodily state and to play a primary role in the regulation of important physiological and endocrinological functions. As the limbic system is also connected with the hypothalamus-pituitary-adrenocortical axis, the right cerebral cortex seems to be primarily involved in the vital survival functions that enable the organism to cope with stress (Shore, 2001).

In accordance with Bowlby's view (1969, p. 344) that the infant's "capacity to cope with stress" is related to certain maternal behaviours, the attachment relationship shapes the development of the infant's cerebral stress-coping-system that acts at an unconscious level, and the infant's representation of bodyself states. The brain, and the right hemisphere in particular, stores an internal model of the attachment relationship containing strategies of psychophysiological regulation that operate particularly in stressful situations. Whether it is integrated or not, the infant's bodyself image thus takes shape in close relationship to the attachment model.

The repertoire of the mother's body language and behaviours seem to be stored not just in the infant's brain but also in the body. This complements neuropsychological studies that now reveal that the right hemisphere (and not the verbal-linguistic one, which develops later), is the site of autobiographical and bodyself memory (Fink et al, 1996; Schore, 1994; Schore, 2003b). Emotional and muscular systems thus have a formative influence on verbal and cognitive development, in contrast to previous theories. Cognitive psychology, seeking to explain psychological processes in terms of processing sensory information, may be losing ground.

The child's capacity to reflect upon emotions and verbalize them offers more options and strategies to monitor emotional tension and cope with stress. The harmonious functioning of the child's right and left hemisphere, resulting from a fulfilling attachment relationship, thus contributes to forming an effective stress-coping system.

CHAPTER 8

The effectiveness of early support

My work with parents and infants is usually short term in nature. It is brief because the infant-parent relationship itself is very young and difficulties can usually be quickly rectified. The earlier the psychotherapeutic work, the more effective it is. This means that the best outcomes will appear very quickly and last longer when the psychotherapeutic work is carried out very early.

The relationship between mother and baby cannot wait for the resolution of past conflicts in the mother or the father through long-term psychoanalytic work, as Stella Acquarone explains in her book *Infant-Parent Psychotherapy* (Acquarone, 2004). A baby develops relatively quickly in the course of active interactions with the mother and father, so a baby cannot be understood outside of these interactions. Neither can the parents be understood without taking these interactions into account.

Psychotherapeutic work with parents and infants requires an integrated and creative use of ideas from child development research, neuropsychological research, infant observations, psychoanalytic literature, theories of infant evolution, psychology, and the arts (for instance, baby massage is the oldest and the most natural of all the healing arts). In my work, I also integrate an Eastern approach to the healing relationship. However, any theoretical background should be continuously filtered by the therapist's creative personality, as this is what enables him or her to truly connect with the parents" and baby's feelings and thus understand them. This makes this kind of work with parents and infants both an art and a science.

What a therapist needs is not the knowledge of a theoretical baby, but the capacity to understand the developing individual baby and his or her changing needs and feelings. This allows the therapist to help parents understand both their baby's cues and needs as well as their own reactions and feelings to their baby's behaviour.

My decision to work with parents and infants and write about this work was led by my strong belief in the extraordinary effectiveness of early support. By detecting the first signs of emotional problems it is possible to treat or prevent a number of *psychosomatic* illnesses. If Andrea's emotional difficulties had been detected early, during her pregnancy or even before pregnancy, her mastitis and all the consequences in the relationship with her baby could probably have been prevented. I did notice some emotional difficulties conveyed through her body language while attending the prenatal classes as an observer and during her labour, but at that stage I had no authority to refer her to a counsellor or therapist or take up psychotherapeutic work with her.

Detecting the early signs of parent-infant difficulties means great savings in personal as well as social costs, because vulnerable infants or children will not need to be constantly referred to medical, social, and educational resources. Moreover, their parents will not anxiously seek constant care.

As a baby's connections are forming in the brain, early support leads to better outcomes than years of treatment later in life. Therefore, it is much shorter than later treatment. Early emotions are imprinted in the brain and in the body; effective early support helps store healthy emotional experiences. Pregnancy and childbirth are a crucial time for parents, since they may bring up unresolved issues that, left untreated, can undermine health and even develop pathological conditions. The potential for therapeutic change before problems are fully internalized is immense and the rewards are satisfying. The case of Andrea and her baby provide a palpable example.

My goal with Andrea was to help her understand the signs of her body/mind, the meaning of her psychosomatic symptom, and their impact on the relationship with her baby. At the same time, I was helping her to understand her baby's body language, needs, and feelings.

Professionals need to understand early signs of problems in babies to allow for their healthy development. In this way, we work for a better society through simple cost-effective early support. Professionals also need to understand signs of psychosomatic disturbance in mothers. This requires sharp observational skills, including the ability to read the mother's body language, symptoms, and her ongoing interactions with her baby. But this is only possible if the professional has an integrative knowledge and thus uses an integrated psychosomatic approach to working with parents and infants.

Andrea's damaged relationship with her mother and her conflicts manifested as mastitis. Observation helps to find associations between bodily aspects, disturbed interactions between mother and baby, and psychoanalytic interpretation. For instance, Andrea's difficulty with breastfeeding, seen as a "symptom", a mind/body strategy to avoid the physical contact with the baby, was consistent with her tendency to leave the baby with others (such as myself or the midwife who assisted in her labour and delivery). Another sign of Andrea's defence against contact was the "faraway" quality of her language and her tendency to speak fast without making eye contact.

Before mastitis signalled to me, as well as to Andrea, the need for change, I received warnings much earlier on about Andrea's need to change the way she felt about her baby, by the fact that she instinctively sought my help. I first met Andrea during my study on birth stories. After telling me her birth story, she expressed her wish to see me again. However, she probably found me too late to prevent mastitis. Her emotions and conflicts, related to a damaged relationship with her parents, were already creating a psychosomatic disturbance. However, we were still in time to repair the difficulties between Andrea and her baby, thanks to my empathic relationship with them and the extraordinary plasticity of the baby's brain and behaviour.

My goal was to lead Andrea to see her primary experience as challenging rather than frightening, and to experience her mothering with creativity and the drive to move forward. The parenting experience may reactivate deep-seated conflicts and thus can bring about extreme vulnerability. The care of a baby may bring about more awareness of past and present conflicts. This is why professionals working with parents-to-be have to do so carefully and sensitively.

A parent's wish for change may be conflictual and unconscious. When Andrea asked me to see her again (stating that "Rosy likes you"), she could see an obvious need for help and thus change. Paradoxically, however, she also actively resisted change, by developing a psychosomatic symptom (mastitis) to distance herself from her anxiety around contact with her baby. Physical contact with her baby through breastfeeding would have reactivated unbearable and painful early experiences. The breastfeeding difficulties proved to be a mind/body strategy to avoid contact with her baby.

Psychoanalytic work in such situations can be long and dangerous, and patients can become stuck in their treatments. The baby's brain is very plastic and needs immediate affective interactions in the present to thrive. The infant's presence in the sessions ensures that parental feelings towards him/her are readily available in the here-and-now for exploration and interpretation. These interactions occur via physical contact between mother and baby. Therefore, psychoanalytic work based only on interpretation could drive parents away from their actual interactions with their baby.

Psychotherapeutic work with parents and infants has to facilitate the change, and this is brought about by the real infant. With their emotional sensitivities, babies often help emotionally inhibited parents to make associations and to better understand their own experiences.

The turning point in Andrea's healing experience was when she made eye contact with her baby for the first time. Rosy's eye contact and its emotional impact created an opening in Andrea's mothering experience. For the first time, she was seeing and getting in touch with her real baby. Pregnancy and birth promote major physical and emotional changes, which can help the parents understand the infant's emotional sensitivity and primitive communications better. If emotional changes are resisted, however, due to frightening anxieties, as in Andrea's case, the parent's empathy for the infant cannot unfold.

This empathic communication between parent and baby can be facilitated by the therapist's empathic relationship with both parents and infant. I believe that this kind of empathic communication within the therapeutic setting greatly determines the outcome of the therapy. The success of the healing relationship or therapy depends more on the personal qualities and experience of the therapist than on theories and techniques. This does not mean that the therapist should not bear in mind findings of infant research, observation, neuropsychology, and other neighbouring disciplines.

The personality of the therapist plays a central part in the healing or therapeutic relationship. Her/his personal make up, cultural and family background, sensitivity, and bodily responses to others" behaviours, are major contributions to the treatment. A therapist needs to be prepared to deal with projective identifications that may feel disturbing and difficult to understand. She/he also needs to consider them as a source of learning, leading them all through the therapeutic process, rather than feeling overwhelmed by them. As I wrote early on, *compassion* is key to connecting with the patient's feelings and needs and to accept and understand the dynamics of projective identification.

In the mother-baby case discussed here, investigations by both Andrea and myself were opened up through transference and countertransference. Over time, I came to understand that Andrea's gesture of handing Rosy to me seemed to validate my function as a container for her anxieties, and to indicate her fear of contact with her baby. That gesture gave me valuable information contributing further to the understanding of her body/mind state. I became the recipient of some of the projections between mother and baby. My compassion and empathy towards mother and baby enabled me to create a *reflective space* for the mother. I made no explicit demands on her and I valued, not judged, her anxieties around her baby.

When I picked up Rosy on the mother's request, I was offering a mirror while also acting as a container for the mother's projected anxieties. In accepting involvement in this extremely delicate process of projective identifications within psychoanalytic work with mother and baby some important elements came to play. These included some of my personal qualities (that enabled me to feel empathy and compassion and to establish a sympathetic relationship with mother and baby), my knowledge of infant research, neuropsychology, observations, developmental psychology, and my work/study experience with parents and infants.

Life experiences also shape the ability to identify or sympathize with others and their different realities. Those who have grown up in a protective or overprotective family, without any curiosity about other people in the world, or who have never travelled and met people, may find it difficult to understand unfamiliar ways of living, which they may tend to judge instead.

When I came to London and began to work at the Birth Unit with parents and infants, speaking little English, I found it quite natural to connect with parents and infants from different cultures. I had travelled extensively, and now I was living in a multicultural city, which, combined with my sensitivity to others, all served to broaden my empathy with infants.

Life experience can motivate a professional to work in a certain field and makes for greater sensitivity. Very often traumatic experiences extend our understanding of human nature and enable us to feel compassion towards our own emotional experiences as well as towards others. It is important and useful to recall such experiences to be able to empathise with infants, especially those with difficulties. Real change brought by therapy can only occur if the therapists let themselves experience what the client's reality feels like.

When I came to London, my difficulty in understanding a new language and adjusting to a new cultural setting made me feel closer to the experience of babies with a difficult start in life. Also, I had to draw upon body language to a great extent, in order to make myself understood and to better understand others' bodily cues.

I communicated less at a verbal and intellectual level, as adults have generally learned to do. This made the infant's body language and sensitivities more accessible to me, and our communications smoother. All these elements actively played a major part in my understanding of Andrea's psychosomatic symptom and her baby's body/mind state and needs.

My awareness and understanding of the experiences of infants was grounded in real thinking about my bodily feelings, rather then simply thinking about thinking. The confidence in myself and compassion towards my own feelings made for greater awareness and understanding. Meditation and the practice of yoga, significant elements in my life experience, have been of particular value in my work with parents and infants as they have provided a practical way to learn to trust myself. I have learnt to feel compassion towards my feelings and life experiences and consider them as a source for better understanding in a therapeutic setting.

Meditation and yoga have helped me exercise my senses and enrich my awareness of other ways of being. They have enhanced my awareness of body and mind and their integration, which is, I believe, essential for an effective therapeutic or healing relationship. Managing a previously unknown language and unknown experiences also allowed me to discover other possibilities of being.

A therapist who is not aware of her/his body feelings, in whom mind and body do not live as a harmonious unity, will not be able to get in touch with the client's own feelings. Besides, she/he will not be able to foster an integration of psyche and soma in the client.

I suggest that a formal training programme of psychotherapeutic work with parents and infants would benefit enormously from being focused on the trainees' broad awareness of their bodyselves and body language in order to help them to become open to all types of communications with parents and infants. This will enable all professionals working with parents and infants to use their own inner resources, and learn from them. By valuing their impressions, sensations, fears, and memories, within an integrated psyche-soma, they are contributing to healthy integration and creativity in the client, which are essential elements in a true healing process.

Effective emotional support in pregnancy, birth, and childcare is aimed at leading the woman to get in touch with her bodyself, as the baby is dwelling in her body and needs a space in her mind as well. I believe that any deep therapy that acts on a mental level and ignores the active role played by the body leads a woman far away from a true connection with her baby. A woman communicates with her prenatal and newborn baby through bodily cues such as breathing, touch, eye contact, movement, and facial expressions, so early parent-infant support has to acknowledge and value these kinds of communication.

I shall adopt the term *"Bow Method"* for a bodyself-image treatment that is aimed at increasing sensory and bodily awareness, thus enhancing the sense of an integrated psyche-soma.

I usually observe both parents and baby to see how they organize their emotional and muscular tension while interacting with each other. Psychotherapeutic work with parents and infants has to be addressed to rhythmic interactions and communication. I use the term Bow Method since rhythm, pace, tuning, and play are fundamental principles of primal interactions and thus social communication. As the musician needs to tune her/his instrument to produce the right notes, so the mother needs to play her own bodyself and body language to tune it to the prenatal and post-natal baby. To do so, her psyche-soma has to be integrated and fluctuating to adjust continuously as pregnancy, labour and mothering progress and her infant's needs change. In a similar way, the therapist has to "feel the music" between parent and infant and attune to their interactions and communications. By providing a "reflective" or "mirroring" space for the parents and infant, the therapist can encourage them to offer such a space to their infant, a space made of attuned communication.

CHAPTER 9

Infant observation

To see the dynamics between parent and infant, we need to be able to observe. Observation is the foundation of research and theory. It is a skill that is sharpened through experience. Infant observation is a valuable training to prepare for psychotherapeutic work with parents and infants and for the work of any health professional concerned with parents and infants. It consists of observing an infant from birth to two years with the mother or father (if he is the main caregiver) in their home, every week for an hour, making detailed notes afterwards, and discussing the observation in a small group. The observer should choose a healthy family.

The purpose of observation is to discern the development of emotions and interactions between mother and baby as well as within the observer, over a period of at least two years. The observer has to learn not to interfere with the dynamics between mother and baby and to bear the strong feelings and anxiety these may induce. By not feeling judged the parent will behave naturally and the observer will be able to witness parent-infant dynamics in a natural setting. Observing parent-infant dynamics is an important experience for the professional who wants to work with parents and infants and thus needs to understand early emotions and early interactions.

The observer should not interfere with the usual activities that take place between infant and parent and has to maintain an attentive, friendly, non-intrusive attitude. The observer has to be continuously aware of her/his own feelings. She/he has to write down the observations in detail soon after and then discuss them in a small group of up to six people with a leader. Each observer presents this written material and they discuss what they have seen, perceived, and felt and their interpretations of it.

As family and observer become familiar with each other, receptivity and trust develop. The purpose of observations is to learn to see and describe processes such as the development of emotions, the emergence of the infant's personality as well as how it moulds the parents' personalities, and the parents' attunement to their baby.

The observer has to be able to cope with different kinds of anxieties rather than fleeing them: some anxieties arise from facing a new experience, whilst some anxieties originate in the inner world of the observer (and are related to her/his past experiences as a baby or to bringing up her/his own children). Anxieties also arise from the infant as well as from the mother.

The observations allow the observer to witness the unfolding of the relationship between mother and baby and explore her/his own emotional responses to this process. They allow the observer to reflect upon her/his own feelings and emotions. By observing, the observer learns to become sensitive to the primitive language of the infant and infer the infant's states from it. She/he also learns to infer the parent's emotional states from her/his body language.

By being passive, receptive, and attentive, the observer learns to withhold acting out, and therefore she/he learns to face anxieties and reflect upon them. The observer learns to tolerate negative feelings (such as anxiety, discomfort, frustration, and anger) that may arise in infants as well as positive feelings (such as love, joy, and gratification).

The observer should be able to see the interplay of transference and countertransference reactions over a period of two years. A clear time for the visits that suits both observer and parents should be established and the observer should respect this schedule without making any alterations. Although the method of observation is not organized by protocols, measures, or codified reporting conventions, it is nevertheless fairly consistent in its approach. Observations take place in a natural setting, either in a group or as a family, on a regular weekly basis for a period of two years. These observations generate written reports, i.e. narrative non-theoretical descriptions of what was observed to happen. A mother-infant observer should identify significant variations in what she or he observes, and to reflect upon the correlations and implications of such variances.

The observation method requires "web thinking" instead of linear thinking. In clinical work this mental frame helps a therapist mould the treatment to the individual's unique needs, rather than locking the parent into a theoretical technique. Observers do not judge or clinically intervene. However, their neutral presence serves to maintain a setting natural and to witness first-hand the mother-baby interactions, which is an important source of data to study their dynamics. The mother banishes any resistance, as she does not feel judged.

My observation/research work in prenatal and post-natal classes shows that the role of a group observer can even be therapeutic due to the observer's capacity to listen and contain the parent's feelings. It also gives meaning to the parenthood experience. Observation is a form of pre-research as well as pre-clinical experience.

An infant observer provides a "reflective space" for the parent, which helps her/him attune to the baby. By providing sympathetic attention, the observer may take on a role that was formerly taken by relatives, parents, friends, and/or neighbours. Nowadays these communities are a resource that cannot be taken for granted. Andrea appeared to be delighted to see me when I visited her the day after she had given birth. She welcomed me in an almost friendly way, as if she had already established a certain relationship with me during the prenatal sessions, even though I had always related to the group she had attended as "just" an observer. I ascribed Andrea's behaviour to my empathic perception of her emotional state, based on my attentive unobtrusive observations of her body language.

A precondition of research should be non-intervening observation to maintain a natural mother-baby setting. Infant observation can be a source of explicit support for isolated mothers and infants, even preventing post-natal depression. Research needs to take place hand in hand with non-intrusive observations, which makes the parent and infant feel safe and confident in a natural environment. Observations should be at the centre of psychotherapeutic training as well as of sensitive yet systematic research methodology.

When I did my masters in Psychoanalytic Observational Studies at the Tavistock Clinic, London, I was undertaking a research/ observational study at the Birth Unit of St John and St Elizabeth Hospital, London. A fundamental part of the master's course was "Infant Observation", which helped me to sharpen my observational skills and to be able to observe the complex interactions between mother and baby and the richness of their body language. I have always had observational skills, but the Infant Observation training helped me to use them more accurately, reflect upon them, and make associations between what I had "observed" and psychoanalytical interpretation.

Observation is the essence of therapy and research. My study experience at the Tavistock, combined with my research/work experience with mothers and babies, and the regular observations of prenatal and post-natal groups at the Birth Unit were invaluable to me in helping heal the relationship between Andrea and her baby. My regular practice of writing down my observations in detail and discussing some of them in sessions at the Tavistock enabled me to convey in words the moment-by-moment changes during mother-baby interactions, as well as to portray the vital interrelationship between the baby's physical and psychological development.

I became able to face my anxieties and primitive feelings and monitor them, learning not to act them out or let them interfere with the process between mother and baby. This training, combined with my meditation and yoga practice, helped me to get in touch with my emotions and use them as a valuable source to understand the development of emotions between mother and baby. Meditation and yoga opened my senses and broadened my awareness of the close relationship between psyche and soma, enabling me to be particularly receptive to the body language of parent and infant, thus to the primitive language of infants. This made communication with infants easier and smoother.

I gradually built compassion towards mothers and babies and in the field of our earliest relationships, as compassion derives from experience within a certain area.

Group observation method: procedure

My observational approach to working with parents and infants became increasingly stronger and systematic. The procedure I followed in my observational study on the Birth Unit was:

Case 1

1. Observing the postural features and body language, such as facial expressions and voice, and taking notes.
    Prenatal yoga class
        Tightened shoulders, neck pulled into shoulders
        Immobile chest and held breathing
        Impediments to emitting primitive sounds during labour rehearsal
        Indicators of emotional state and bodyself perception
        Repeated patterns, not occasional postural display

2. Listening to the woman's experience during prenatal support classes.

3. Listening to the birth story two or three days after delivery.
        Subjective experience of birth–perception of pain, length of labour, etc.
        Life and pregnancy events: i.e.
            Abandoned by her partner at two month's gestation
        Kind of birth:
            Emergency caesarean: pelvis stopped dilating
            Inhibiting anxiety
            Baby as active participant in the labour process, able to sense the mother's tension and contribute to the progress of labour

4. Observing the mother's handling of her newborn baby.
    Breastfeeding class
        Same chest-shoulders-neck features observed during
        pregnancy
        Never smiling
        Lack of eye contact and vocal interactions with her
        baby
        Fairly slow movements while handling her baby
        Always sitting in the corner and behind the group

    Indicators of mother's depression and low self-confidence
        Not connected with her baby
        Baby low-weight, sluggish flat behaviour, motionless,
        staring at the ceiling, no vocalizations
        *Indicators of the relationship between the baby's
        development and the mother's emotional state and body
        language*

    Baby massage class
        Undressing and placing the baby on the floor as
        something fragile
        Insecure touch: use of fingertips instead of whole
        hand
        Looking at other mothers with unease rather than
        focusing on herself and her baby
        Lack of eye contact and talking or vocalizing with her
        baby
        Same chest-shoulders-neck feature observed
        prenatally
        Rigid arms and hands
        Fragmented movements

5. Two months later
        Mother displays more secure gestures and firm touch
        while breastfeeding and massaging her baby
        More frequent eye contact and tactile and verbal
        interactions
        Smiling with eye contact

Indicators of increased confidence in mothering and enjoyment of the relationship with her baby, and more harmonious bodyself
Baby appears more responsive and active, increases his movements on being massaged, smiles, and vocalizes
Weight-gain
Indicators of improving health condition and baby's relationship with the mother's state, self-confidence, bodyself, and overall well-being

6. Identifying significant variations in what I observed and reflecting upon the correlations and implications of such variances-formulating hypothesis for research.

7. Implications for parent-infant psychotherapeutic work addressed to rhythmic interactions and communication. Parents communicate with their baby through bodily cues such as breathing, posture, touch, eye contact, movement, and facial expressions. Therefore, early support for parents and infants has to value these kinds of communication. I suggest that any therapy that acts on the mental level and ignores the active role played by the body leads parents far away from a true connection with their baby.

Case 2

Prenatal
I have observed Jane in prenatal yoga classes for about four months. Her posture appears rigid, her shoulders closed and stiff without showing the tiniest movement when the teacher suggests that she breath deeply. Her neck is pulled down into her shoulders. Her eyes move around and do not appear to be focusing on her inner self. Her facial muscles look equally tense. Her insistent questioning about labour is accompanied by an evident expression of fear.

Labour
Labour lasted two hours. Midwives say she was extremely anxious during labour. Anxiety can affect the progress of labour in two opposite directions: either lengthening or shortening it.

Post-natal
She feels unbearable pain inside her breast while breastfeeding. She

looks very tense while talking about her breastfeeding experience and the way of holding her baby looks very insecure. The baby is very tiny.

Two months later
Attending a weekly baby massage class.

Mother's shoulders look less tense. New facial expressions blossom on her face and a feeling of well-being has gradually started shining in her complexion and smile. Her touch while massaging her baby looks more confident. Baby is evidently gaining weight.

Observed links
Prolonged emotional/muscular tension (especially shoulders and chest) during pregnancy may have affected the functioning of the breast muscle and sucking rhythm coordination, and consequently the baby's growth. There is a correlation with two other cases in which emotional conflict and psychosomatic disturbance have been identified as the possible basis for mastitis.

Giving meaning to what has been observed
The special contact between mother and baby during massage helps the mother relieve her tension and gain in self-confidence, and thus boosts a more positive attitude to her bodyself and to her baby. The case also reveals the power of the group and shared experience with other mothers as containment and mirror.

Tuning to the melody

One of the most important aspects of infant observation is the impact it has on the observer's emotional life. It is this change, I believe, that is the powerful source of the healing relationship with parents and infants. This is why it is a fundamental preparation for clinical work. I also want to highlight some aspects that are familiar to the Eastern approach to psychotherapeutic work with parents and infants as described in Chapter 6.

Infant observation stirs up powerful feelings in the observer, during the interactions between mother (or father) and an infant.

Such intensity of feeling experienced in an ordinary setting prepares the observer for being able to cope with the strength and depth of feelings arising in more disturbing circumstances, such as that of the mother and baby presented in this book.

All of us experience extremely intense feelings in the presence of a newborn baby. Birth and death are major life events. In newborns we see the most vulnerable state of a human. This can make infant observation a hard experience, but also valuable, as it prepares the observer for re-experiencing the intense feelings of primal life. These feelings need to find a "reflective space" in which to be thought about and elaborated. The observer needs to "tune" in to her/his feelings, to listen to the inner melody, and in doing so, tune into the mother-baby interactions. The capacity to "feel", to "listen" to the body's feelings, to "think" about them, and to give them "meaning" leads to an integrated psyche-soma in the observer and the prospective clinician.

Observation is obviously never neutral. Observation is based on values, assumptions, and constructions of experience. "It is an epistemological fallacy to think that we can stand outside what we observe, or observe without distortion, what is alien to our experience" (Levenson, 1972, p. 8). The experience of observation is subjective, but it is important to highlight the risk of the observer using a particular theory to see things that are not there. Awareness of the distortion that can arise is fundamental for "objective evaluation" (Trowell, 2002). What is seen should be reflected upon and used to clarify some theoretical concept or to reinforce intuitions. For instance, seeing the interactions between mother and baby during the observations gave me more evidence that emotion manifests itself through bodily states, an area in which I have long been interested.

Observing involves experiencing emotions. It is the emotional experience that enables the observer to understand more about the emotional life and non-verbal behaviour of infants and young children and reflect upon relationships and their origin.

Houzel (1999) described three aspects of "receptivity":

1. Receptivity at a perceptual level, of things that are manifest and can be objectively seen, such as gestures, vocalizations, changes in vocal tone, and changes in muscle tone.

2. Emotional and empathic receptivity, which enables the observer to experience to some degree what the infant and parents may be experiencing.

3. "Unconscious receptivity", which displays itself in countertransference. As I wrote earlier on, this third aspect is extremely important, as it is a valuable source of information about the observer's states and about what is going on in the observation or the clinical setting.

Observation requires the observer the capacity for introspection, thus to look within him or herself and be aware of his or her internal processes as well as of those observed (Waddell 1988). The capacity to infer the mother's and infant's internal states, however, requires the capacity to see their non-verbal behaviour and body language.

The closeness to the infant and mother arouses in the observer intense feelings deriving from her/his own infancy. I see the exposure to these intense feelings as an opportunity for growth, enabling the observer to master his or her feelings in clinical work later on, rather than being frightened by them and fleeing them.

Trowell and Rustin (Trowell, 2002; Trowell & Rustin, 1991) have written about the importance for the observer to be able to learn from experience and to tolerate and share confusion and uncertainty. This is an important principle of Eastern approaches to psychotherapeutic work, as discussed above.

My infant observation experience combined with my research/ observation work on the Birth Unit enabled me to contain the anxieties evoked by the mother and infant difficult relationship illustrated in this book. I was able to observe what was happening in my bodyself as well as in the mother and baby. No doubt, the practice of yoga and meditation had enhanced my awareness of the bodyself and my ongoing feelings, allowing me to experience the emotions aroused during the observations with an integrated psyche-soma.

The work of an observer and a therapist are similar in many ways. Like a therapist, the observer has to note, experience, and think about what he or she is experiencing. Not opening oneself up to inner feelings prevents the observational and therapeutic work from being effective.

The emotional body should work in synchrony with the reflective space in a psyche-soma that is integrated. When this is possible, within the observer and the clinician, she/he will be able to see things from an integrated perspective. When the observer is open to experiencing feelings, she is able to bear not knowing rather than being taken by the impulse to control events and assuming according to a theory. This concept seems to me very close to Eastern approaches to observation and to the healing relationship, which I have written about in Chapter 6. The capacity to face the unknown with an "openness of heart" is the basis for both genuine listening and creative thought.

You can think about feelings if you can truly experience them with all your body. This kind of mental frame requires a capacity to tolerate anxiety, uncertainties, fear, helplessness, and discomfort. A therapist needs these capacities to make the psychotherapeutic work effective.

The capacity to experience and reflect belongs to an integrated psyche-soma, and once the observer has acquired this capacity, he or she will find it extremely valuable in clinical work with parents and infants. I want to emphasise the crucial importance of this, as, through mirroring, the parent will develop the capacity to experience and reflect upon the infant's experience, which is fundamental for an integrated psyche-soma. The infant's development will benefit enormously from the parent's integration of psyche and soma.

Barrows (1999) described how parent-infant work is closely linked to infant observation, and frequently cites Winnicott. The use of infant observation in parent-infant work encourages parents to be observers of their children, to really see them and think about their experience, rather than about an ideal child.

At times it may be difficult for the observer to not take action, but it is valuable training for being "present" without intervening. I have written extensively in this book about the importance of being present in the therapeutic setting and healing relationship. "Doing" precludes the opportunity to "be" and reflect (Tanner, 1999), while "doing nothing" means "being present", or "being yourself". This is central to Eastern psychotherapy, while Western disciplines tend to "do", i.e. intervene with a particular theory or technique. "Doing nothing" allows the observer and prospective professional to be able to listen to inner feelings, to connect with the parent and infant, and thus to experience empathy without "acting".

This ability to experience emotion and then to contain it is at the heart of observational experience as well as of effective clinical work. Observation helps the observer to get in touch with inner emotions and to get to know parts of his or her personality. Writing about them strengthens the connection to them and enhances bodyself-awareness. As I have discussed above, the personality of the professional working with parents and infants plays a major role in the healing relationship with the client. The infant observation seminar group takes on the crucial role of containing the observer's anxieties and provides a space for thinking about the observer's inner feelings as well as reflecting on the mother-infant dyad. The ability to master anxieties enables the observer to reflect over time.

By discussing what occurred, the seminar group setting may help give meaning to the infant's experience, which helps the observer to get more in touch with the infant. Barbara Segal (2003) considers the importance of the seminar group to be in offering a reflective space, which helps the observers to understand their personal reactions to the observations. The group acts as a "mirror" for the observer, as it reflects back the observer's emotional states.

The group offers the observers the opportunity to compare the infants within the seminar, thus to learn about diversities of culture. This leads to a less judgemental attitude, which is fundamental to getting in touch with mother and infant and with the client in clinical work. Through the group, the observers become aware of how different each child's experience is.

An important aspect of observation is that the experience of it brings to awareness "the uniqueness of each couple, how each baby develops at its own pace and relates to its mother in its own way" (Bick, 1964, p. 254). Acknowledging this uniqueness is also important for the future clinician to prevent a rigid application of theory and technique. The awareness of diversity should help the observer to look at the infant and parent-infant relationship for what they are.

As I undertook infant observation, and become aware of the diverse realities provided by the infant observation seminar in multicultural London, I began to let go of stereotypes. This enabled me to be less judgemental and understand more deeply cultural differences and similarities. The research/observation work I was carrying out on the Birth Unit in London put me in contact with a number of parents and infants from a diversity of cultures, making the experience of infant observation far richer. On the other hand, my experiences at the Birth Unit benefited enormously from experiencing infant observation. The capacity to understand differences allowed me to truly connect with the individual experiences of parents and infants, which is at the heart of the healing relationship, as we have seen in the case described in Chapter 5.

Bick (1964) wrote that the experience of infant observation would help the clinician to understand children's non-verbal communication and play. Emotions are embodied in bodily states and observation allows the observer to see this. Infant observation has allowed researchers and clinicians to enjoy a more realistic understanding of infant development, and a better awareness of their capacities (Trevarthen, 1998). It has brought about important changes in analytic thinking and practice, with more of a focus on cultural and interpersonal aspects than on intrapsychic processes. This new viewpoint has also brought raised awareness of the importance of the environment in infant development.

My cultural background offered me the perspective to develop an approach focused on psychosomatic integration. From this viewpoint, as I carried out my research and parent-infant work, I was able to discover the enormous richness in infant observation by seeing the ongoing interactions between the infant's inseparable psychic and somatic processes in her/his development.

Acknowledging the baby's positive capacities has had an important impact on analytic theories and psychotherapeutic work, and has led to the belief in the baby's own capacities to recover. The baby has become active participant and amazing contributor to the parent-infant psychotherapeutic work.

I suggest that any practitioner working with parents and infants would benefit enormously from the experience of infant observation in their training. To understand the parent-infant relationship we need to be able to observe. Having the opportunity to experience intense emotional feelings that have to be processed and reflected upon enables any professional with a concern for parents and infants to "connect" with them, which is at the very core of understanding.

CHAPTER 10

Conclusions

In this book, I have explored the philosophical framework of dualism and its formative influence on the development of psychoanalytic psychosomatics. I have highlighted Winnicott's work on the psyche-soma as a break from the dualistic tradition that, unlike the work of existential analysts, resides within an object-relations perspective. I have built on Winnicott's work, on Pines' thinking about a woman's unconscious use of her body, and on Kleinian and post-Kleinian visions, to highlight the benefits of baby massage classes as what I believe should be an integral part of psychotherapeutic work with parents and infants.

My exploration of certain philosophical and theoretical issues within psychoanalysis has been in the service of "building a home" for clinical work with parents and infants and for infant observation settings. Such a home should be built upon the three following principles:

1. It should combine a *phenomenological perspective* based on a vision of a unified psyche-soma, with an *object relations perspective*, in order to draw connections between individual infant and individual adult experiences.

2. It should focus equally on health and illness and acknowledge the continuum between health and illness. The understanding of the process of psychosomatic illness rests on the exploration of the embodiment of psychosomatic health and illness.

3. It should be inspired by Eastern psychotherapeutic approaches. I propose a meeting between Western psychotherapeutic approaches–grounded in the need for enhancing awareness of self–and Eastern traditions, which emphasise a larger kind of awareness, compassion, and equanimity, as a continuously available source of clarity and health. Building awareness of oneself through meditation is a potential basis for working with others. By a fuller opening of the heart and liberation of oneself from the distortions of a confused mind, psychotherapeutic work allows for a true connection with the client, based on empathy and compassion. By opening up and listening to inner feelings and emotions, the therapist offers a mirror to the client for opening more fully.

The concept of abeneficial function of psychosomatic symptoms, such as mastitis, is central to the development of such a home. A psychosomatic symptom is seen here as an essential signal to the therapist as well as the patient, indicating the need for change and the path through which it may occur. Acknowledging the continuum between health and illness is important to understand the subjective meaning and function of symptoms, as they inform the therapist of a divorce between psyche and soma.

Early experiences of body movement, touch, and of maternal handling become inscribed upon the body and tend to elude elaboration in words. I have assumed that these early experiences impinge on the development of a grounded bodyself and of an integrated psyche-soma. My contention is that, in adult life they shape the way a mother uses her body in interacting with her baby. Inadequate or damaging experiences of handling and loving are here seen as altering the harmony and unity of the psyche-soma–body and self are split–and body is experienced as an object rather than the venue of the self, which results in psychosomatic symptoms.

Andrea's apparently "perfect pregnancy" and her attention directed mostly outwards, which I noticed during the prenatal classes, seem to have been a sign of an altered psyche-soma. An inward focus is one of the most universal psychological changes in pregnancy, and Winnicott (1962a) describes this beautifully. The direction of a pregnant woman's interest turns from outwards to inwards. She slowly comes to believe that the centre of the world is in her own body. The last part of pregnancy is usually dominated by a turmoil that always seems to be adaptive. The goal for this turmoil is for the woman to mobilize all her emotional energy in making the tremendous adjustment to parenthood and bonding with her baby. Her self-questioning and inward focus help her to find those special capacities that she needs to parent the baby successfully (Klaus, Kennell, & Klaus, 1996). In Andrea there seemed to be a denial of self-questioning at work.

Brazelton and Cramer (1990) see the anxiety that is characteristic of a pregnant woman as something that mobilizes the energy necessary for the vast work ahead and the development of attachment. The regressive state of the pregnant woman seems to be adaptive and enables her to rediscover her primary language, identify herself with her baby through mirroring, and thus understand her cues and establish a rhythmic dialogue (Raphael-Leff, 1993).

The mother's attitude to her body and self determines whether she resists this healthy regression during pregnancy or lets her energy be mobilized. Her relationship with her bodyself, subject to continuous adjustments during pregnancy, shapes the woman's sensitivity to the foetus' cues and establishes an intimate form of communication. The ability to attune to her own bodily rhythms and thus to those of the baby allows the mother to nurture an image of the baby that is closer to the real individual baby (Sansone, 2004, p. 120). This attunement is expression of a psychosomatic integration.

The clinical illustration presented in this book is an example of ways in which the mother's engagement with an infant massage group may either act directly to sustain a good sense of bodily in-dwelling and/or serve as a bridge to early bodily experiences, through a mirroring process induced by contact with infant.

Like Winnicott and Pines, I have endeavoured to consider the whole issue of a mother's relationship to her "embodiment", thus to her use of her body, when psychosomatic symptoms are concerned, for example breastfeeding problems such as mastitis. Mastitis is commonly considered to be primarily a medical problem by midwives, obstetricians, and other health professionals. I found that mastitis was not Andrea's central problem but a "symptom", a mind/body strategy to avoid physical contact with her baby, which would have stirred up unbearable anxieties. This was consistent with her tendency to put others in charge of holding her baby. With the help of Winnicott's work and contributions from psychoanalytic infant observations, we are in a position to develop our understanding of embodiments of psychological health as well as illness.

I underpin in this book the importance of acknowledging activities involving the body, as they may convey either pathological or beneficial overtones. We are aware that when a client offers an account, we have to attend to the "colouring" of this in order to make progress in inferring meaning. This colouring should more widely include the client's body language, such as Andrea's breastfeeding posture, her neutral facial expression, fast speed of voice, far-away language, and lack of eye contact, viewed within an object-relations perspective. Associations with accounts of physical experiences, for example the knee problems that allowed Andrea to give up ballet, with somatic symptoms such as mastitis, might reveal the client's use of her body to deal with emotional issues and the functioning of her psyche-soma.

In the same way, Andrea's frequent showers, an excuse to leave the baby with a "supply mother", may be seen within an object-relations perspective. For example, having repeated showers may be related to sensuality, to compensating for impaired early experiences of maternal touch and holding and to reaching towards a sense of psycho-physical well-being, whereas paradoxically her somatic symptoms may be the manifestation of a damaged psyche-soma. The particular meaning of a client's engagement in a certain activity as well as any psychosomatic symptoms will only fully emerge in clinical exploration. I never investigated Andrea's arguments with the obstetrician concerning "nutrition", but this left me thinking of the link between eating behaviours and emotional nourishment in our earliest life.

On the same line as Winnicott's vision of the psyche-soma, I have argued that somatic aspects of self-expression and communication play a useful and essential part in everyday life. In this book I refer to their major role in the mother-infant relationship. Infant massage in particular, offered me an interesting setting for observing Andrea's way of handling her baby, her gestures, and body language. Their significance was inferred through making connections in a psychoanalytic setting.

I consider infant massage to be an vital part of psychotherapeutic work with parents and infants, as this is when physical experience is accessible to thought, which links to actual memories or to "memories-in-feeling" (Klein, 1957, p. 180) and can be elaborated in object-relations terms. I have considered how infant massage may help restore a sense of psychosomatic well-being in the mother as well as aid its evolution in the baby. For Winnicott such well-being is home for a true self, a source of authenticity and enjoyment.

Winnicott saw the body in health as a dwelling place, inseparable from a sense of self. As well as bringing into play a rich source of material for psychoanalytic exploration, infant massage may be directly involved in gaining or regaining that sense of "psychosomatic indwelling" to which Winnicott refers, which in health characterized our earliest months of life and without which we cannot feel truly whole.

The clinical illustration presented in this book highlights the active contribution of the infant in psychotherapeutic work with infants and parents, as it brings into play a rich source of material for psychoanalytic exploration. With their emotional sensitivity, babies often help emotionally inhibited parents to make links and to understand better their own experience.

The infant's presence allows the therapist to witness the infant's own contribution to the problem, to appraise his or her development and to share his or her achievements with her parent. It seems that within their first two and a half years or so, before internal representations become firmly established, infants retain a remarkable behavioural flexibility (Hopkins, 1992). The identification with their baby enhances the parents' capacity to regress and re-experience early relationships.

As Hopkins writes, the therapist contribution remains essential, even if it is simply to provide a "holding environment" in Winnicott's sense, or "containment" as described by Bion. Whatever the orientation of the therapist, the family know that they are listened to, that they are not alone with their troubles and that there is hope for change. The internal representation of a critical, undermining parent may thus temporarily be displaced by the representation of an approving, supporting one, and so allow a new pattern of interaction to be initiated.

Over time, I came to understand that Andrea's recurrent gesture of handing Rosy to me seemed to validate my function as a container for her anxieties and fears around contact with her baby. That gesture brought into play a rich source of material for exploration. I provided an additional "reflective space" for the mother in particular and sympathetic attention to the mother and her baby, without making explicit demands on her, for example, for routine information about the frequency of feeds or the intake of medicine. The baby was implicitly defined as of interest; through my gesture of picking her up on the mother's request, the mother's anxieties about her baby were valued, and not judged. I was increasingly becoming a transference object, an ideal "supply mother", on which inferences in the therapeutic process depend heavily.

It is in this "reflective space" that a baby massage teacher has the potential to provide a containing function, by allowing space for the parent to find the difference between mindful and mindless touch. Though massaging baby Rosy occasionally, to show Andrea some massage movements when difficulties occurred, I was offering a mirror while being a containing, mindful object to the mother's projected anxiety. The practice of massage, my containing function, and the mother's increased psychosomatic well-being established a circular process that stimulated relatedness, vitality, and sense of bodyself in the baby, which in turn enhanced the mother's confidence in handling her baby.

In my book *Mothers, Babies and their Body Language* I explain:

The experience of touch with the baby may mobilize feelings such as anxiety, sorrow, and anger, and make a parent react with defence mechanisms and tightening of muscles. However, working through the contact with the baby can be a crucial path to exorcising ghosts from the past. It consists in a working through in the context of the present relationship, through self-investigation and observation, rather than a distant past. Merely going back to the parents" primary experiences at such a delicate time as pregnancy and birth may increase the suffering and worry and drive parents away from their relationship with their body, which consists mainly of bodily rhythmic interactions. [Sansone, 2004, p. 14]

There are many opportunities for growth and renewal and it is a principal aim of effective support to make parents aware of these possibilities. The experience of touch makes parents and their overwhelming feelings related to early experiences more likely to turn into something positive. Bonding can repair the traumas they may have suffered as children. The bond is experienced as a source of security and joy for both parents and baby and as a pleasurable experience.

This kind of support based on the "contact experience", which enhances a parent's ability to respond to the baby's needs, is vital in decreasing the risk of post-natal depression. Baby massage is an effective tool that can complement psychotherapeutic work.

Selma Fraiberg (1980) considered that, like all short-term therapies, psychotherapeutic work with infants and parents is focused, and the focus is on the development of the infant who is always present in the sessions. The infant's presence ensures that parental feelings towards him or her are readily available in the here-and-now for exploration and interpretation. This means that symptoms in the infant as well as in the mother can best be treated by treating the infant-parent relationship, rather than by treating either infant or parent separately. Fraiberg saw the symptomatic infant as the victim of negative transference, haunted by "ghosts in the nursery". In the same way, the mother's symptom, such as mastitis, may be related to her early experiences. The primary focus of the work is on understanding the parents' transference to their baby, rather than on understanding their transference to the therapist. This awareness in fact strengthened Andrea's ability to change things in the present.

It is relevant that infant-parent psychotherapy, especially in the case of a parent with psychosomatic symptoms, should not remain the exclusive territory of psychotherapists. Considering a psychosomatic symptom as solely a medical problem does not help to improve the infant-parent relationship, and can cause more stress in the mother as it emerges. Collaboration with staff of a general practice or baby clinic may be an essential step. Midwives and health professionals working with parents and infants should be trained to acknowledge the emotional aspect of breastfeeding problems and to develop an integrated approach to psychosomatic problems. Experienced practitioners with parents and infants from many professional backgrounds can be enabled to enrich their work with the additional understanding that infant-parent psychotherapy brings.

I also underpin the importance for all professionals working with parents and infants to experience infant observation during their training, as observation is fundamental for understanding. The experience of intense feelings aroused during the observation that have to be processed and reflected upon enables any professional with a concern for parents and infants to "sympathise" with them, which is at the very heart of understanding. Working with infants may arouse in professionals intense anxieties related to their infancy, to which they may react with defensive mechanisms, such as avoiding them. The experience of infant observation allows professionals to have a more realistic knowledge of the individual infant, thus of their inner child, and to "feel" and elaborate their emotions rather then fleeing them.

The potential for therapeutic change before problems are fully internalized is immense and the rewards are correspondingly satisfying. My major focus was on Andrea's capacity to interpret the function and meaning of her psychosomatic symptom and the use of her body, so that she could become able to withdraw her negative projections from her baby and so facilitate the infant's development.

During a follow-up conversation we had two years after the short-term therapy, I received important evidence from Andrea about the beneficial potential of psychosomatic symptoms when they lead to the understanding of their meaning. In regard to her first breastfeeding experience, Andrea commented:

With Rosy I got mastitis. They gave me antibiotics but I knew that I didn't need them. I was stressed out. I think that the midwives were not skilled to handle breastfeeding difficulties, as they didn't see the link with emotions, stress or anxiety.

Then she told me about her second and third little girl (delivered at the same hospital):

With my second girl I developed slight mastitis. They were giving me antibiotics but I decided to use homeopathy and I eventually became able to breastfeed. With the third one I had no problems. She is eight months and I'm still breastfeeding. I do believe that emotions play an important part in breastfeeding and in labour.

I was quite struck when, without been questioned, she stepped back to her first labour:

My body was confused. I did want a baby but I was not prepared. It was like facing an examination paper, something I had to achieve. I was screaming and acting with fear. In yoga classes they say you should scream in labour to let go, but I don't think this is necessary. During my last birth I was quiet.

In Andrea's idealized pregnancy, confused labouring body, and mastitis, we can see a dysfunction of the interaction between psyche and soma, probably linked to a primal dysfunctional use of psyche and soma. Central to this book is that intergenerational working models are embodied; they may act through the body by developing a symptom. Breastfeeding problems can be seen as the visible expression of a turmoil that has been going on throughout pregnancy and is rooted in early life.

I assume that if Andrea had had the possibility to explore some very painful memories and feelings during early pregnancy, she might have been increasingly able to address her current problems and perhaps, to prevent mastitis. Andrea's use of her psychosomatic symptom alerted me to an area of heightened emotionality, which I might otherwise have missed if had not seen the link. For a person who has experienced insufficient containment, a psychosomatic symptom may serve to bolster her "second skin" at some cost to emotional possibilities but also possibly warding off a very real danger of breakdown. In Andrea's case, the breakdown could have been triggered, for example, by physical contact with her baby and the anxieties related to it.

Winnicott believed that a split between psyche and soma was a recurrent risk in adult life. Pregnancy and birth, like any turning point in an individual's life, can be a critical opportunity. When, in adult life, a sense of in-dwelling in the body is impaired, then, like Winnicott's patient (1949), we may suffer from feelings of depersonalization, unreality, and a falseness in living. I saw in Andrea's "idyllic" pregnancy, confused labour, and mastitis a poor sense of true self. The development of a psychosomatic illness is conceived in this clinical case as an expression of an impaired sense of bodyself, or, in other words, a lack of psychosomatic integration.

Transference and countertransference: the important tools

I want to highlight the importance of two important tools in the psychoanalytic and healing relationship: transference and countertransference. The transference is re-enactment in the here-and-now of past experiences, bringing what has hitherto been repressed into consciousness in a safer setting. It provides important informative material for analytic work as it reveals the repressed past by re-living it.

Transference enables the therapist to proceed. In a mother-infant consultation is an important source of information. Fraiberg (1980) suggested that positive transference of the mother should be used to explore the baby's world and his or her own difficulties, while the negative transference of the mother provides information about her relationship with the therapist. The therapist has to be able to understand the non-verbal communication of the infant, such as the lack of aliveness or inert body, as in Andrea's baby. The baby is in fact an active participant in the consultation, and is able to re-enact and communicate with his or her body, hands, eyes, and movements–her earliest relations through transference.

The aim of using the transference material is to explore and then to free the potential for effective communication and healthy development of the parent-infant relationship. From birth, the infant shows a unique capacity to actively participate in complex social and affective interactions. Since the parent-infant relationship is very young, the infant's brain is very plastic and the difficulties have not yet become entrenched, psychotherapeutic work with parents and infants need not be a long process.

Countertransference is the therapist's response to the patient (Brazelton, Koslowsky, & Main, 1974; Stern, 1974). The therapist's feelings induced by both the parents and the baby provides important insights, clues, and links, which guide understanding. However, such feelings may cause extreme anxiety or feelings of rejection in the therapist, who may wish to be rid of this quickly by, for example, referring the parent to another professional colleague. This reaction is usually linked to identification with internal objects in the mother or in the baby that the therapist cannot cope with. It is of the utmost importance for the progress of psychotherapy that the therapist explores her/his feelings and what has induced them, in order to use those feelings to provide insights in understanding the infant-mother relationship.

A common reaction in a psychotherapist working with parents and infants is feeling so caught up in the parents" inner world that the infant is ignored and left alone. This response may be an indication of denial of the baby's existence and identification with the parents, as the therapist's own past is re-enacted. The resistance of the therapist may express itself through rationalizing that the mother-infant psychotherapeutic work only concerns working with the mother's representation of the baby. This reveals problems in the process of identification in the therapist's earliest life.

Psychoanalytic treatment will help the therapist to recreate the inner infant and acknowledge her/his infant-mother relationship. I suggest that such psychoanalytic work in the patient has to focus also on a mind-body work, which enables the therapist to re-discover his or her own infant primitive/body language, in order to be able to understand the infant's language and needs. Yet as psychoanalysis does not change our actual past, but creates a new attitude to it through re-elaboration and bodily reliving of it, unresolved emotions linked to early life (such as anger for not having been held), may undermine the therapist's confidence in countertransference. The therapist's ability to help parents and infants may then be weakened.

I consider that meditation has the potential to complement psychoanalytic work for therapists, as it can strengthen their ability to cope with emotions and enhance their trust in their bodily feelings. The therapist is enabled to listen to the sensory, visceral, cognitive, and emotional organs as sources of nonverbal information. Meditation allows for stronger connection and insights. Regular practice can enable a therapist to trust his or her insights into the internal world of mother, father, and infant, which means to connect with their emotions and experience compassion. Parents will learn to trust their own insights, bodily feelings, and language, which will enable them to perceive the cues and to connect sensitively with the needs of their baby. Parents will learn, by seeing compassion in the therapist and through a mirroring process, to feel compassion towards themselves and their baby.

References

Abram, J. (1996). *The Language of Winnicott*. London: Karnac Books.

Acquarone, S. (2004). *Infant-Parent Psychotherapy. A Handbook*. London: Karnac Books.

Ainsworth, H., Blehar, M., Waters, E., & Wall, S. (1978). *Patterns of Attachment: A Psychological Study of the Strange Situation*. Hillsdale, NJ: Lawrence Erlbaum.

Anderson, G. C. (1991). Current knowledge about skin-to-skin (kangaroo) care for preterm infants. *Journal of Perinatology 11*: 216-226.

Anisfeld, E., Casper, V., Nozyce, M., & Cunningham, N. (1990). Does infant carrying promote attachment? An experimental study of the effects of increased physical contact on the development of attachment, *Child Development, 61*: 1617-1627.

Barnard, K. E., & Brazelton, T. B. (Eds.) (1990). *Touch: the Foundation of Experience*. Madison, CT: International Universities Press.

Barrows, P. (1999). Brief work with under-fives: a psychoanalytic approach. *Clinical Child Psychology and Psychiatry, 4*(2), 187-199.

Bermúdez, J. L., Marcel, A., & Eilan, N. (Eds.) (1995). *The Body and The Self*. Cambridge, MA: MIT Press.

Bick, E. (1964). The experience of skin in early object-relations. In: M. Harris Williams (Ed.), *Collected Papers of Martha Harris and Esther Bick* (pp. 114-119). Perthshire: Clunie Press, 1987.

Bick, E. (1968). The experience of the skin in early object relations. *International Journal of Psychoanalysis, 49*: 184-186.

Bion, W. R. (1948). Experiences in groups: I and II. *Human Relations, 1*: 314-320, 487-496.

Bion, W. R. (1962a). *Learning from Experience*. London: Heinemann.

Bion, W. R. (1962b). Container and contained. In: W. R. Bion (Ed.), *Elements of Psychoanalysis*. London: Heinemann. [Reprinted London: Karnac Books, 1984].

Bowlby, J. (1969). *Attachment and Loss, Volume 1: Attachment*. New York: Basic Books.

Bowlby, J. (1979). *The Making and Breaking of Affectional Bonds.* London: Tavistock.

Brazelton, T. B. (1983). *Infants and Mothers. Differences in Development.* New York: Delta Press.

Brazelton, T. B. (1995). Fetal observations: could they relate to another modality, such as touch? In: E. Field (Ed.), *Touch in Early Development* (pp. 11-18). Mahwah, NJ: Lawrence Erlbaum.

Brazelton, T. B., & Cramer, B. G. (1990). *The Earliest Relationship: Parents, Infants, and the Drama of Early Attachment.* London: Karnac Books.

Brazelton, T. B., Koslowsky, B., & Main, M. (1974). The origins of reciprocity: the early mother-infant interaction. In: M. Lewis, & L. Rosenblum (Eds.), *The Effects of the Infant on its Caregiver* (pp. 49-77). New York: Wiley.

Bruner, J. (1983). From communicating to talking. In: Bruner, J. (Ed.), *Child's Talk: Learning to Use Language* (pp. 23-42). Oxford: Oxford University Press.

Collins, D. (1996). Attacks on the body: how can we understand self-harm? *Psychodynamic Counselling, 2*(4): 463-475.

Damasio, A. (1999). *The Feeling of What Happens. Body and Emotions in the Making of Consciousness.* London: Harcourt Brace.

Descartes, R. (1644). *Principles of Philosophy.* E. Anscombe, & P. Geach (Trans.). London: Nelson.

Eliot, L. (2001). *Early Intelligence: How the Brain and the Mind Develop in the First Years.* London: Penguin.

Feldman, R., Greenbaum, C., & Yirmiya, N. (1999). Mother-infant affect synchrony as an antecedent of the emergence of self-control. *Developmental Psychology, 35*: 223-231.

Field, T. M. (1977). Effects of early separation, interactive defects, and experimental manipulations on infant-mother face-to-face interaction. *Child Development, 48*: 763-771.

Field, T. M. (1985). Attachment as psychobiological attunement. In: T. Field, & M. Reite (Eds.) *The Psychobiology of Attachment and Separation* (pp. 415-450). New York: Academic Press.

Field, T. M. (1990). Neonatal stress and coping in intensive care. *Infant Mental Health Journal, 11*: 57-65.

Field, T. M. (Ed.) (1995). *Touch in Early Development.* Mahwah, NJ: Lawrence Erlbaum.

Field, T. M., Shanberg, S., Scafidi, F., Bauer, C., Vega-Lahr, N., Garcia, R., Nystrom, J., & Kuhn, C. (1986). Tactile/kinesthetic stimulation effects on preterm neonates. *Paediatrics, 77*: 654-658.

Fink, G. R., Markowitsch, H. J., Reinkmeier, M., Bruckbauer, T., Kessler, J., & Heiss, W. D. (1996). Cerebral representation of one's own past: neural networks involved in autobiographical memory. *Journal of Neuroscience, 16*: 4275-4282.

Feinman, S. (Ed.) (1992). *Social Referencing and the Social Construction of Reality in Infancy.* New York: Plenum Press.

Fraiberg, S. (1974). Blind infants and their mothers: an examination of the sign system. In: Lewis, M., & Rosenblum, L. (Eds.), *The Effect of the Infant on its Caregiver* (pp. 215-232). New York: Wiley.

Fraiberg, S. (1980). *Clinical Studies in Infant Mental Health: The First Year of Life.* London: Tavistock.

Freud, S. (1901). *Fragment of an Analysis of a Case of Hysteria. Standard Edition Volume 7.* (pp. 1-22). Freud, S. (1953-1974), 1953.

Freud, S. (1905d). *Three Essays on the Theory of Sexuality, Standard Edition Volume 7* (pp. 130-243). Freud, S. (1953-1974), 1953.

Freud, S. (1911b). *Formulations on the Two Principles of Mental Functioning, Standard Edition, Volume 12* (pp. 218-226). Freud, S. (1953-1974), 1958.

Freud, S. (1923b). *The Ego and the Id, Standard Edition, Volume 19* (pp. 12-66). Freud, S. (1953-1974), 1960.

Freud, S. (1953-1974). *The Standard Edition of the Complete Psychological Works of Sigmund Freud, Volumes 1-24.* J. Strachey. (Trans. and ed.). London: Hogarth Press.

Freud, S., & Breuer, J. (1893). *Studies in Hysteria. Standard Edition Volume 2* (pp. 3-305). Freud, S. (1953-1974), 1955.

Gergely, G., & Watson, J. (1996). The social biofeedback theory of parental affect-mirroring. *International Journal of Psychoanalysis, 77*: 1181-212.

Goleman, D. (1996). *Emotional Intelligence.* London: Bloomsbury.

Gross, J., & Levenson, R. (1997). Hiding feelings: the acute effects of inhibiting negative and positive emotion. *Journal of Abnormal Psychology, 106*(1): 95-103.

Harlow, H. F., & Harlow, M. K. (1962). Social deprivation in monkeys. *Scientific American, 207*: 136-144.

Hegel, G. (1807). *Phenomenology of the Spirit*. A. V. Miller (Trans.). Oxford: Clarendon Press, 1977.

Heidegger, M. (1927). *Being and Time*. J. Macquarrie, & E. S. Robinson (Trans.). New York: Harper & Row, 1962.

Hess, E. H. (1975). The role of pupil size in communication. *Scientific American*, 233: 110-119.

Hopkins, J. (1990). The observed infant of attachment theory. *British Journal of Psychotherapy*, 6: 457-469.

Hopkins, J. (1992). Infant-parent psychotherapy. *Journal of Child Psychotherapy*, 18: 5-17.

Houzel, D. (1999). A therapeutic application of infant observation in child psychiatry. *International Journal of Infant Observation*, 2 (3): 42-53.

Isaacs, S. (1948). The nature and function of phantasy. In: M. Klein, P. Heimann, S. Isaacs, & J. Riviere (Eds.) *Developments in Psychoanalysis* (pp. 67-121). London: Hogarth Press.

Klaus, M. H., Kennell, J. H., & Klaus, P. H. (1996). *Bonding. Building the Foundations of Secure Attachment and Independence*. London: Cedar Press.

Klein, M. (1935). A contribution to the psychogenesis of manic-depressive states. In: *Love, Guilt and Reparation and Other Works* (pp. 262-289). London: Hogarth Press, 1975.

Klein, M. (1946). Notes on some schizoid mechanisms. In: M. Klein, 1975.

Klein, M. (1948). The development of a child. In: *Contributions to Psychoanalysis 1921-1945* (pp. 13-67). London: Hogarth Press (1965).

Klein, M. (1957). Envy and gratitude. In: M. Klein, 1975.

Klein, M. (1975). *The Writings of Melanie Klein, Vol. 3 Envy and Gratitude and Other Works 1946-1963*. London: Hogarth Press. [Reprinted New York: Basic Books, 1975, and Free Press 1975, 1984].

LeDoux, J. (1996). *The Emotional Brain. The Mysterious Underpinning of Emotional Life*. New York: Simon & Schuster.

Levenson, E. (1972). *The Fallacy of Understanding*. New York: Basic Books.

Liedloff, J. (1986). *The Continuum Concept. In Search of Happiness Lost*. London: Penguin.

Likierman, M. (1993). He drew my attention to my great gift for understanding children... Some thoughts on Sandor Ferenczi and his influence on Melanie Klein. *British Journal of Psychotherapy*, 9 (4): 444-455.

Lyons-Ruth, K. (2000). I sense that you sense that I sense..: Sander's recognition process and the specificity of relational moves in the psychotherapeutic setting. *Infant Mental Health Journal, 21*: 85-98.

McDougall, J. (1974). The psychosomatic and psychoanalytic process. *International Review of Psychoanalysis, 1*: 437-454.

McDougall, J. (1989). *Theatres of the Body: A Psychoanalytical Approach to Psychosomatic Illness*. London: Free Association Books.

McKenna, J. J. (1986). An anthropological perspective on the sudden infant death syndrome (SIDS): the role of parental breathing cues and speech breathing adaptation. *Medical Anthropology,* 10: 9-53.

Miller, L., Rustin, M., Rustin, M., & Shuttleworth, J. (Eds.). (1989). *Closely Observed Infants*. New York: Harper & Row.

Montague, A. (1978). *Touching*. New York: Harper & Row.

Murray, L. (1997a). Postpartum depression and child development. *Psychological Medicine, 27*: 253-260.

Murray, L. (1997b). The early mother-infant relationship: a research prospective. *Infant Observation, 1*: 80-90.

Murray, L. and Stein, A. (1991). The effects of postnatal depression on mother-infant relations and infant development. In: M. Woodhead, & R. Carr (Eds.), *Becoming a Person. A Reader* (pp. 144-166). London: Routledge.

Murray, L., & Trevarthen, C. (1985). Emotional regulation of interactions between two-month-olds and their mothers. In: T. Field, & N. Fox (Eds). *Social Perception in Infants* (pp. 177-197). Norwood, NJ: Ablex Publishing.

Newman, L. F. (1980). Parents' perception of their low-birth-weight infants. *Paediatrician, 9*: 182.

Olds, D., & Cooper, A. (1997). Dialogue with other sciences: opportunity for mutual gain. *International Journal of Psychoanalysis, 78*: 219-225.

Papousek, H., & Papousek, M. (1987). Intuitive parenting: a dialectic counterpart to the infant's integrative competence. In: J. D. Osofsky (Ed.), *Handbook of Infant Development*, 2nd ed., pp. 669-720. New York: Wiley.

Perry, B. D., Pollard, R., Brakely, T., Baker, W., & Vigilante, D. (1995). Childhood trauma, the neurobiology of adaptation and 'use dependent' development of the brain: how states become traits. *Infant Mental Health Journal, 16* (4): 471-291.

Phillips, A. (1988). *Winnicott*. London: Fontana.

Pines, D. (1993). *A Woman's Unconscious Use of her Body. Psychoanalytical Perspective*. London: Virago Press.

Piontelli, A. (1992). *From Foetus to Child. An Observational and Psychoanalytic Study*. London: Tavistock/Routledge.

Raphael-Leff, J. (1993). *Pregnancy. The Inside Story*. London: Sheldon Press.

Reite, M., & Field, T. (Eds.), 1985 *The Psychobiology of Attachment and Separation*. New York: Academic Press.

Rolls, E. (1999). *The Brain and Emotions*. Oxford: Oxford University Press.

Ruggieri, V. (1987). *Semeiotica di Processi Psicofisiologici e Psicosomatici*. Rome: Il Pensiero Scientifico Editore.

Rustin, M. J. (1989). Observing infants: reflections on method. In: L. Miller, M. Rustin, M., Rustin, & J. Shuttleworth (Eds.), *Closely Observed Infants* (pp. 52-87). New York: Harper & Row.

Rustin, M. (1991). *The Good Society and the Inner World: Psychoanalysis, Politics And Culture*. London: Verso Books.

Sansone, A. (2002). The mother's body image: attitude to her body-self and its relationship with the foetus life. *International Journal of Prenatal Psychology and Medicine, 14*: 163-175.

Sansone, A. (2004). *Mothers, Babies and their Body Language*. London: Karnac Books.

Sauls, D. J. (2002). Effects of labour support on mothers, babies, and birth outcomes. *Journal of Obstetric, Gynaecologic, & Neonatal Nursing, 31*(6), 733-741.

Scafidi, F., Field, T., Schanberg, S., & Bauer, C. (1990). Massage stimulates growth in preterm infants: a replication. *Infant Behaviour and Development, 13*: 167.

Schore, A. (1994). *Affect Regulation and the Origin of the Self: The Neurobiology of Emotional Development*. Hillsdale, NJ: Lawrence Erlbaum.

Schore, A. (2000a). Foreword. In: J. Bowlby, *Attachment and Loss Series, Vol. 1: Attachment* (p. xi). New York: Basic Books.

Schore, A. (2000b). Attachment and the regulation of the right brain. *Attachment and Human Development*, 2: 23-47.

Schore, A. (2001). The effects of a secure attachment relationship on right brain development, affect regulation and infant mental health. *Infant Mental Health Journal*, 22: 7-66.

Schore, A. (2003a). *Affect Dysregulation and Disorders of the Self*. New York: Norton.

Schore, A. (2003b). Minds in the making: attachment, the self-organizing brain and developmentally oriented psychoanalytic psychotherapy. In: J. Corrigall, & H. Wilkinson (Eds.), *Revolutionary Connections: Psychotherapy and Neuroscience* (pp. 7-51). London: Karnac Books.

Segal, B. (2003). Anxieties, questions and technical issues in beginning observation. *International Journal of Infant Observation*, 5 (3): 11-23.

Seigal, D. J. (1999). *The Developing Mind: Towards a Neurobiology of Interpersonal Experience*. New York: Guilford Press.

Spitz, R. (1945). Hospitalism: an inquiry into the genesis of psychiatric conditions in early childhood. *Psychoanalytic Study of the Child*, 1: 53-74.

Stern, D. (1974). Mother and infant at play: the dyadic interaction involving facial, vocal and gaze behaviour. In: M. Lewis, & L. Rosenblum (Eds.), *The Effects of the Infant on Its Caregiver* (pp. 187-213). New York: Wiley.

Stern, D. (2000). *The Interpersonal World of the Infant: A. View from Psychoanalysis and Developmental Psychology* (2nd ed). New York: Basic Books.

Suzuki, D. T. (1949). *Introduction to Zen Buddhism*. London: Rider.

Tanner, K. (1999). Observation: a counter culture offensive. *International Journal of Infant Observation*, 2 (2): 12-32.

Thompson, M., & Westreich, R. (1989). Restriction of mother-infant contact in the immediate postnatal period. In: I. Chalmer,

M. Enkin, & M. Kierse (Eds.) *Effective Care in Pregnancy* (pp. 13-28). Oxford: Oxford University Press.

Thoman, E. B., Ingersoll, E. W., & Acebo, C. (1991). Premature infants seek rhythmic stimulation, and the experience facilitates neurobehavioral development. *Journal of Developmental Behaviour Paediatrics, 12:* 11-18.

Trevarthen, C. (1980). Foundations of intersubjectivity: development of interpersonal and cooperative understanding of infants. In: Olson, D. (Ed.) *The Social Foundations of Language and Thought* (pp. 316-342). New York: Norton.

Trevarthen, C. (1998). When the beholder is beholden, the infant's psyche may be strong. *International Journal of Infant Observation*, 1(3): 105-116.

Trevarthen, C. (1999). Musicality and the intrinsic motive pulse: evidence from human psychobiology and infant communication. *Musicae Scientae Special Issue, 1999-2000. Rhythms, Musical Narrative, and the Origins of Human Communication,* pp. 157-213. Liege: European Society for the Cognitive Sciences of Music.

Trevarthen, C. (2001a). Intrinsic motives for companionship in understanding: their origin, development and significance for infant mental health. *Infant Mental Health Journal, 22:* 95-131.

Trevarthen, C. (2001b). The neurobiology of early communication: intersubjective regulations in human brain development. In: A. F. Kalverboer, & A. Gramsbergen (Eds.), *Handbook on Brain and Behaviour in Human Development* (pp. 841-882). Dordrecht, Netherlands: Kluwer Academic.

Trevarthen, C. (2002). Origins of musical identity: evidence from infancy for musical social awareness. In: R. MacDonald, D. J. Hargreaves, & D. Miell (Eds.), *Musical Identities*, (pp. 21-38). Oxford: Oxford University Press.

Trevarthen, C. (2003). Neuroscience and intrinsic psychodynamics: current knowledge and potential for therapy. In: J. Corrigall, & H. Wilkinson (Eds.), *Revolutionary Connections: Psychotherapy and Neuroscience* (pp. 53-78). London: Karnac Books.

Trevarthen, C., Kokkinaki, T., & Fiamenghi, G. A. (1999). What infants' imitations communicate: with mothers, with fathers, and with peers. In: J. Nadel, & G. Butterworth (Eds.), *Imitation in Infancy* (pp. 128-185). Cambridge: Cambridge University Press.

Tronick, E., Als, H., Adamson, L., Wisu, S., & Brazelton, T. B. (1978). The infant's response to entrapment between contradictory messages in face-to-face interaction. *Journal of the American Academy of Child Psychiatry, 17*: 1-13.

Trowell, J. (2002). The wider applications of infant observation. In: B. Kahr (Ed.), *The Legacy of Winnicott* (pp. 79-88). London: Karnac Books.

Trowell, J., & Rustin, M. (1991). Developing the internal observer in professionals in training. *Infant Mental Health Journal, 12*: 233-345.

Turner, J. (2000). *On The Origins of Human Emotions*. Palo Alto, CA: Stanford University Press.

Turp, M. (1998). In sickness and in health? Psychoanalysis and psychosomatics. *Psychodynamic Counselling, 4* (1), 3-16.

Van Rees, S., & de Leeuw, R. (1987). *Born too Early: The Kangaroo Method with Premature Babies*. Video. Heythuysen, Holland: Stichting Lichaamstaal.

Waddell, M. (1988). Infantile development: Kleinian and post-Kleinian theory, infant observational practice. *British Journal of Psychotherapy, 4* (3): 313-328.

Williams, M. (Ed.) (1978). *Collected Papers of Martha Harris and Esther Bick*. Perthshire: Clunie Press.

Winnicott, D. W. (1931). *Clinical Notes on Disorders of Childhood*. London: Heinemann.

Winnicott, D. W. (1949). Mind and its relation to the psyche-soma. In: D. W. Winnicott, 1958a.

Winnicott, D. W. (1952). Anxiety associated with insecurity. In: D. W. Winnicott, 1958a.

Winnicott, D. W. (1953). Transitional objects and transitional phenomena. In: Winnicott, 1958a.

Winnicott, D. W. (1958a). *Collected Papers: Through Paediatrics to Psychoanalysis*. London: Tavistock.

Winnicott, D. W. (1958b). Maternal reverie. In: D. W. Winnicott, 1958a.

Winnicott, D. W. (1960a). Ego distortion in terms of true and false self. In: D. W. Winnicott, 1965.

Winnicott, D. W. (1960b). The theory of the parent-infant relationship. In: D. W. Winnicott, 1965.

Winnicott, D. W. (1962a). Ego integration in child development. In: D. W. Winnicott, 1965.

Winnicott, D. W. (1962b). The child in health and crisis. In: D. W. Winnicott, 1965.

Winnicott, D. W. (1963). From dependence towards independence in the development of the individual. In: D. W. Winnicott, 1965.

Winnicott, D. W. (1965). *The Maturational Processes and the Facilitating Environment*. London: Hogarth Press. [Reprinted London: Karnac Books, 1990.]

Winnicott, D. W. (1966). Psychosomatic illness in its positive and negative aspects. *International Journal of Psychoanalysis, 47*: 510-515.

Winnicott, D. W. (1967). The concept of a healthy individual. In: C. Winnicott, R. Shepherd, & M. Davis (Eds.) *Home Is Where We Start From*. Harmondsworth: Penguin, 1986. [New York: Norton, 1990.]

Winnicott, D. W. (1971). *Playing and Reality*. London: Tavistock, 1991.

Winnicott, D. W. (1987). *Babies and their Mothers*. London: Free Association Books.

Winnicott, D. W. (1988). *Human Nature*. London: Free Association Books.

Winnicott, D. W. (1991). *The Child, the Family and the Outside World*. London: Penguin.

Wolman, W. L., Chalmers, B., Hofmeyr, G. J., & Nikodem,V. C. (1993). Postpartum depression and companionship in the clinical birth environment: a randomised, controlled study. *American Journal of Obstetrics and Gynaecology, 168*: 1388-1393.

Yamada, H., Sadato, N., Konishi, Y., Muramoto, S. Kimura, K, Tanaka, M., Yonekura, Y., Ishii, Y., & Itoh, H. (2000). A milestone for normal development of the infantile brain detected by functional MRI. *Neurology, 55*: 218-223.

Index